The Accidental Tour Guide

The Accidental Tour Guide

Adventures in Life and Death

MARY MOODY

**SIMON &
SCHUSTER**

London · New York · Sydney · Toronto · New Delhi

A CBS COMPANY

THE ACCIDENTAL TOUR GUIDE
First published in Australia in 2019 by
Simon & Schuster (Australia) Pty Limited
Suite 19A, Level 1, Building C, 450 Miller Street, Cammeray, NSW 2062

10 9 8 7 6 5 4 3 2 1

A CBS Company
Sydney New York London Toronto New Delhi
Visit our website at www.simonandschuster.com.au

A catalogue record for this
book is available from the
National Library of Australia

Cover design: Lisa White
Cover artwork: 'In the Greenhouse' by Angela Mckay;
www.ohkiistudio.com
Typeset by Midland Typesetters, Australia
Printed and bound in Australia by Griffin Press

The paper this book is printed on is certified
against the Forest Stewardship Council®
Standards. Griffin Press holds FSC chain
of custody certification SGS-COC-005088.
FSC promotes environmentally responsible,
socially beneficial and economically viable
management of the world's forests.

To David Hannay, Isabella Hannay and
Margaret Travis

Contents

Part 2: After David

'You know that place between sleep and awake, that place where you still remember dreaming? That's where I'll always love you . . . That's where I'll be waiting.'

J.M. Barrie, *Peter Pan*

Prologue

In those first few seconds between the soft nothingness of sleep and the inevitability of waking, I have completely forgotten. Lying on my right side, I open my eyes and see David's fine profile, as ever. His smooth olive skin; his silvery hair on the pillow.

Then I remember. He died last night, just after eight o'clock. He's still here with me, in our bed of more than four decades. I slide my left hand across the space between us and onto his belly. Still warm; just a little bit warm. It's late March and very cold at our farm in rural Yetholme, but our bed's well covered with woollen blankets and eiderdown. I reach up and touch his icy cheek. It's true then. It really did happen.

I feel disoriented. It's only natural: these are the first moments of a very different life. I can't begin to imagine what that life looks like from here. I know that I must get up and start the day. There's so much to do, to organise, to settle. There are thirteen people staying at the farmhouse – our four children, some of their partners and most of their children. We need to call the doctor (the death certificate), the palliative care team (to notify), the undertaker (the body), the Anglican minister (a plot in the local cemetery), close family members (David's brother and sister), and dozens of friends and neighbours. We have a funeral to plan.

I kiss his forehead; it feels so strange. I need tea, proper leaves in a teapot. Our bedroom opens onto a wide hallway heading down to the kitchen. David's huge portrait is on the wall opposite our doorway; he looks melancholy, eyes downcast. That's how the artist saw him; that's how he saw himself.

There's a small child wearing pyjamas in the hallway, skipping and singing to himself. My grandson Owynn. Oblivious to my presence, 'Granddad's dead, Granddad's dead' is Owynn's repeated chant. He was here in our room last night; everyone was crying. This surely must be his three-year-old way of processing that collective deluge of grief. Poor little chap, I hope he's not permanently traumatised. Yet his song has made me smile, almost laugh, reassuring me that life will somehow go on.

He's hungry so I make toast while the kettle boils. I throw some small logs into the wood stove, tickle the embers alive.

One by one, family members emerge from the bedrooms that also open to the wide hallway. There are children and teenagers sleeping on various sofas and blow-up beds. Nobody is feeling chatty; they look at me, wondering how I am today. We all go through the motions of breakfast, trying to ease into this very strange new day.

I'm fine really; numb but functioning. Cuddling kids, letting cats and dogs in and out the back door. Wondering if anyone remembered to shut the latch of the chicken shed last night. Probably not.

I take my second cup of tea back to bed, to where David still lies. He brought me tea in bed every morning we were together for, perhaps, the last thirty years. During our first decade together I was usually up before him, wrangling babies and small children. But after that phase he cheerfully took over, coming back to bed himself with a coffee and the newspaper. It occurs to me that this will be our last morning in bed together, ever. I drink my tea slowly, deliberately. I must never forget these last few hours.

A decision is made to keep David here until later today, when our daughter Miriam's husband and her four sons will arrive from Adelaide. I want the boys to see their grandfather one last time, at the farm, in his own bed. They have spent all their summer holidays here with us for fifteen years. Running wild. It's their place of happy memories and cousin time.

I don't need to make any of the difficult calls; our adult children swing into action organising everything. I am allowed to float, to ask questions, to make suggestions, to add a name to the list. I can't believe we didn't discuss any of this until now. In spite of the last two years of certainty, knowing it would end this way, we have never discussed one single aspect of what will happen in the hours, the days, the weeks and the months that will follow the death. I never brought it up with David; he never brought it up with me.

I am so appreciative and overwhelmed by this love and support. Our children working together to make all this easier for me, just as they have worked as a team these last four days to support their dying father. I am grateful.

It will take me four years to feel like myself again. The 'old' me needs to stand aside and allow the remade version of myself to emerge. However, in those few days between the death of my husband and his funeral, I have no foreboding of the difficult path that lies ahead.

PART 1

Losing David

1

The beginning

I was twenty-one and full of ambitious enthusiasm when I first met David Hannay. It was 1971 and I had just graduated as a graded journalist following a three-year cadetship at the *Australian Women's Weekly*. I had a boyfriend my own age, but he'd recently headed off to London and I was saving up to join him. In order to accumulate the money I needed for this journey, I left my reliable magazine job for a pay rise in the publicity department of the television station Channel 9; this day job also allowed me to have a night gig as a barmaid at my local, the Mosman Hotel.

When I first started at Channel 9, my plan was to quickly escape the publicity role for that of news reporter, even though at that time there were only two women television journalists in Sydney, both at the ABC. I wanted to take my

3

news reporter training a little further into uncharted territory. I was not beautiful but I had an open face and a ready smile. I had long red hair which I wore hanging straight in the fashion of the day, belying the fact that my hair was naturally even curlier than Nicole Kidman's locks in the film *BMX Bandits*. It took hours of laborious winding of wet hair around my head to achieve this smooth style. I also wore thick make up to cover my freckles, and black false eyelashes – another must-have fashion of the sixties.

Not long into my new job, an unusual looking chap walked into the small publicity office. He was balding with long blond-streaked hair and a bright red beard that reached halfway down his front. I noticed his intense brown-black eyes as he politely introduced himself, telling me he was a part of an independent production company making a weekly family show called *The Godfathers*.

'Where did you spring from?' he asked. I laughed and told him about my journalism background and because I'd never seen the program he offered to take me onto the set in Studio 2 to watch an episode being taped. I was immediately fascinated by the process of television production – and him.

That evening I reported to my mother that I'd met a man called David at work that day, saying he looked a bit like a garden gnome. He wore a 'trademark' outfit of pale blue denim jeans, matching jacket, tall leather boots and a silk scarf around his neck. All he needed was a pointed hat.

For me it was not love at first sight; I was still besotted with my absent high school boyfriend and excitedly told David

I was planning to fly to London as soon as possible, so I would probably only work at the station for six months or so.

I also mentioned I was keen to try TV news reporting and to my amazement he immediately organised an audition for me with the station's popular current affairs program, *A Current Affair* with Mike Willesee. It didn't dawn on me at the time that he was trying hard to impress me. Somehow I thought myself to be sophisticated but looking back I realise I was completely unworldly in the ways of men.

David would pop into my office every morning for a chat, interrupting my daily media deadlines by sitting on the edge of my desk drinking coffee. It was fortunate that my boss was an easygoing bloke. David was dismayed when my audition for the program came to nothing, although the 'soft news' story I had put together for them was actually played on the program the following week.

'Women aren't really welcome in the newsroom,' the news director explained, not bothering to let me down gently.

'We had a woman once and she was nothing but trouble. In the end she took off with one of our best reporters.'

Imagine using that language to an aspiring job applicant in this day and age. I was disappointed – but not really surprised.

David asked me out but I was so busy doing my barmaid gig six nights a week I had no time left for socialising – by Sunday, my night off, I was always worn out. A few weeks later he trailed around after me at the Channel 9 Christmas party, where I had what we now know as a show business

#MeToo moment. I was invited by one of the corporate secretaries go with her by taxi to a nearby motel for an after-party. Despite my naiveté I soon realised it was a small, exclusive party. In a hotel room filled with bottles of champagne there were two female secretaries, three rather scary senior executives and me, the new girl. It was a set-up. I had a nasty head cold and, snuffling and sneezing, managed to beg off, catching a taxi home at great cost to my junior wage. The following Monday morning David appeared at my desk asking where I'd vanished to – he said he'd been searching for me at the original party for hours until he gave up and went home.

I told him the 'executive set-up' saga and he was incensed. Later I discovered that David loved nothing more than to be incensed; to be enraged. He was a bit of a drama queen. He'd been an actor in both film and television in Australia for several years in his early twenties and before that a child radio actor in New Zealand. In his late twenties he switched to the production side of the business.

I do sometimes wonder if I'd stayed at that party and co-operated in the 'fun' with the executives, would it have advanced my 'girl reporter' television ambitions? I doubt it – the two young secretaries were never promoted beyond their 'personal assistant' status.

The development of my relationship with David happened slowly and naturally. He was eleven years older and he took me under his wing. I enjoyed his company and his attention. Sometimes we ate lunch together in the work canteen and eventually, on one of my Sunday nights off, we went out on our first date. We smoked some dope and drank some beer and I stayed the night in his small bedsit. I had never made love to an adult male before and I really liked it. My boyfriend from schooldays was lovely but not driven sexually. He had addiction problems and I'd been supporting him financially before his parents gave him the plane ticket to London for his twenty-first birthday. He was a talented artist and they hoped it would inspire him to get started on his career.

David, I soon discovered, had been married for ten years and had had several other relationships, both before and after the marriage. He was separated from his wife but he failed to mention to me on that first crazy night we spent together that his ex was in an advanced stage of pregnancy. I was given that startling news several days later when he cornered me in the canteen and told me excitedly that his estranged wife had just given birth to a baby boy. I can't remember exactly how I felt, but I must have been confronted and confused by the revelation.

Looking back at that time of my life, I acknowledge that it was absolute madness. I was making significant decisions and choices at such an early age with little (or no) real-life experience. What was I doing sliding into a serious relationship with a still married but separated man who had just become a father? How did David manage to convince me to meet his wife and baby Tony? Which I did. Tony was adorable and I struck up a sort of friendship with his wife, guilelessly offering to give her a break from mothering for a few hours every Sunday so that David could spend time with his son. My parents were perplexed when we turned up for lunch the following Sunday with a baby in a basket on the platform shelf of David's hardtop MGB. (Babies didn't have protective car seats or seatbelts back then.) I would cuddle Tony at the lunch table and feed him bottled breast milk that his mother had expressed for his weekly 'family outing'.

David had a very powerful and persuasive personality. He was intense and quite obviously determined to hang onto me and our new relationship. It's just as well I loved babies.

We'd been living together for several months in David's little bedsit when my old boyfriend flew home from the UK to try to woo me back. It didn't work. I felt terrible about betraying him as I had dearly loved him, but it had become a hopeless situation. My attempts to save enough money to join him were futile: almost every week he phoned me at work, reverse charges, asking me to urgently send him money. He hadn't even tried to find a job and as fast as I was saving, it was all going overseas, undoubtedly to pay for his drugs as well as his rent. Very sadly, he died in Paris in his thirties of an accidental drug overdose.

My parents were both journalists and between them earned an excellent income. They had both been staunch members of the Communist Party and at various times my father used this as an ideological excuse not to enter the property market. His political convictions were not the only reason we lived in a small rental flat for most of my childhood. A heavy drinker and gambler, Dad simply had no desire to spend his salary on a mortgage. I could barely believe that by the age of twenty-two I was in a committed relationship with an older (still married) man and that my name was next to his on the title deeds of a house.

This was how it all began. How could I have imagined that the man who had reminded me of a garden gnome would be my life partner for forty-three wild and (mostly) wonderful years? How could I have known that, from being a lowly PR junior, I would spend much of my career writing about gardening, leading people on botanical treks in the Himalayas and being a TV presenter on a national gardening show?

2

Diagnosis

MARCH 2012

Dying has never been something David's contemplated. The first doctor to mention the word 'cancer' is given a cordial but firm lecture after the uncomfortable specialist tried his best to deliver the worrying results of the recent tests, and explain the possible implications.

After a lengthy pause.

'Well, Henry, this is certainly not part of my plan,' David begins.

He's seventy-two, a member of a long-lived family with a justifiable expectation of a similar life expectancy for himself. Although he smoked tobacco in his twenties and enjoys smoking dope with his film friends a couple of times a year, he's never been much of a drinker and has been an obsessive exercise junkie for at least the past twenty years. In the beginning, he power-walked two hours a day then, when his knees started to suffer, he started swimming laps of the local pool for the same length of time six days a week. He looks and feels extremely healthy and greets the discovery of his cancer with anger and disbelief. Mostly anger.

'I'm planning to continue working until my mid-eighties, then perhaps do a few character cameo roles in my friends' films, then I contemplate working on my memoirs when I get into my nineties. Having cancer is certainly no part of my agenda,' he states firmly.

Poor Henry: there's not much he can say to this proclamation. He writes referrals to various Sydney specialists and tells us about the excellent cancer-care facility at Bathurst, a town about twenty-five minutes' drive from our farm, where David will need to go for his chemotherapy.

Driving home, we are curiously quiet. I'm not sure why. Neither of us has considered the possibility of cancer, even though the first gastroscopy failed to yield a result because of a large obstruction in his oesophagus. There had been a clue, recounted to me by David at the time, when the anaesthetist sat with him in the recovery room, patting his hand reassuringly. He obviously had an insight into what was going on; what had blocked the scope from entering the stomach. He was being kind.

I now realise we've been practising denial and avoidance in the weeks and months leading up to this bleak diagnosis. Maybe it's the same for most people. We have an inbuilt sense that something isn't quite right but because the progress of the disease is so well hidden away in the depths of the body, this 'gut feeling' can be brushed off; ignored. It's the opposite of being a hypochondriac. Many people don't seek help simply because they don't want to know – they are so fearful of being diagnosed with something frightening, they'd rather pay no attention to the symptoms and carry on as if nothing is awry.

Many years ago when David was in his early forties, overweight and feeling sluggish, he became a regular at our local medical practice. He was quickly diagnosed with pre-type 2 diabetes and was determined to turn it around by changing his diet and starting an intense exercise regime. It worked a treat: he looked and felt so much better and all his follow-up results showed that lifestyle changes had made a profound difference. However, he needed constant reassurance and often requested even more tests. Our doctor jokingly referred to him as 'the worried well', which he was – at that stage. It was unusual for a bloke: statistics show men tend to be slow to seek medical attention, even if they have genuine concerns. This is partly why we're now astounded by this gloomy diagnosis.

There had been plenty of clues. David often stood up from the table part-way through a meal, tapping the middle of his chest as if trying to dislodge something. He described it as reflux, which he had been treated for with medication for several years. He didn't – not once – describe it has 'having trouble swallowing'. Those three easy words, if uttered six months earlier, may have meant the difference between life and death. Thinking about it now, I'm gobsmacked. David's a filmmaker, a storyteller and a brilliant communicator. Yet he couldn't find a simple phrase to describe his discomfort. When I asked how he was feeling, he would usually reply, 'I feel like shit', which of course means nothing. With hindsight, we kick ourselves.

Our rural GP, too. A gentle man with great doctor–patient rapport. Early in David's treatment I pop in to see him about some trivial health problem of my own, and he eyeballs me, asking, 'Does David blame me?'

It's rare indeed for a doctor to even hint at a possible failure, but this man is the exception. He's obviously taken David's diagnosis hard and is beating himself up for not suggesting a gastroscopy a little earlier.

'David only blames himself, certainly not you,' I reassure him.

Then I describe to him our late-night conversations about the lack of communication that resulted in the problem not being recognised sooner. David is angry, that's for sure, but he certainly isn't directing his anger at anyone in the medical profession. Not yet, anyway.

There's nothing to be gained by pointing the finger or laying blame. We all wish we'd noticed or paid more attention. We all wish the cancer cells hadn't spread. But life isn't about what happens to you, it's about how you deal with it. I want to cope bravely, with lots of love and a smattering of humour. It will take me a long time to reach this point.

3

My crazy family

BALMORAL BEACH, 1950s

Apart from the age difference, David and I also came from completely different backgrounds. He was a New Zealander from a conservative establishment background and had been educated at private boarding schools. His grandfather had been a prominent lawyer and his uncle was the Solicitor-General. David was the rebel of the family, running away from home as a teenager to work as a merchant seaman, then settling in Australia to try and launch a career as an actor. When I later met his parents and siblings I liked them tremendously, but the way he'd described them had convinced me that I wouldn't be to their liking at all. My own childhood couldn't have been more dissimilar.

As a child you don't have a sense of your family being abnormal or, as it's called these days, dysfunctional. It wasn't until I grew up, left home and looked back that I realised my family really was very offbeat in many ways. We were a blended family. My father had been married and widowed, leaving him with two children, Jon and Margaret. He then married my mother who was ten years younger than him and together, nine years later, they had three offspring – my older brother Dan, then me and a second girl named Jane. Our home life was chaotic as both parents were feisty, argumentative chain-smokers and alcoholics who held down high-powered and stressful jobs. I just thought all families were like mine. Our small flat near the beach was a battleground, as my parents warred mostly about money, politics and sex. My dad was a serial philanderer and it created a permanent air of tension in the family home. He was completely hopeless with money. Most weekdays he would start drinking at eight in the morning at the early-opening pub on his way to work. At the weekends he spent a lot of his salary betting on the horseraces, phoning his illegal bookie and becoming more and more belligerent if he was on a losing streak. My parents' arguments were volatile and sometimes physical, and I spent many nights in bed listening to the ructions and feeling vulnerable and insecure.

Yet some aspects of my childhood were marvellous. Living at Balmoral Beach was enchanting and the family paradox was that my parents loved books, music and good food. On weekends when he wasn't gambling my father would burrow into his deep armchair with an ashtray and flagon of claret by his side, reading the books he'd then review for the next weekend's newspaper. He was the editor but also liked to do the book reviews. My mother would be ironing, drinking sweet sherry from a huge tumbler while pressing all Dad's starched white work shirts and our school uniforms. Beethoven would be on the record player and from the kitchen the Sunday roast would fill the room with delicious aromas. Those are very real and happy memories. If my parents started to brawl after lunch my brother Dan and I would retreat to the beach where we always felt happy and free. Invariably when we returned in the early evening they would be fast asleep, only getting up, badly hungover, in time for the seven o'clock news.

My brother Dan and I seemed destined for journalism. Dan started a cadetship at the *Daily Mirror* and a few years later I joined the *Australian Women's Weekly*.

When I started on the magazine I adored the world of these sophisticated and ambitious women journalists: the stylish clothes they wore, their outrageous humour and steely wit, and the way they smoked and gossiped at their desks. We worked hard to get that magazine out on deadline; in those days it really was a weekly and contained terrific articles about Australian women achieving great things; nothing like the celebrity gossip rags of today.

My father encouraged me to specialise: to find a niche that I really enjoyed and to become well known for writing about it. My training at the magazine was very general, as we were given an opportunity to write about everything from fashion to news. It was a good grounding but I was still casting about for my niche.

When I met David and was introduced to his world of television and film production, my career veered in that direction. After Channel 9, I worked in a variety of roles, from a year at *TV Week* magazine to a role at the Australian Film Commission promoting the short films of young directors, some of whom have gone on to become internationally famous (such as Phil Noyce and Gillian Armstrong). I wrote about Australian filmmakers and locally made films for an international cinema journal and felt very much a part of the 1970s surge in the emerging Australian film industry. I thought I'd found my niche.

While I was making my way in this career I was also having David's children. Before meeting him, the idea of becoming a mother was not high on my to-do list. Like my older sister, Margaret, who had managed to convince a specialist in Canada to tie her fallopian tubes when she was in her late twenties, our difficult childhood had convinced me that being a parent was just too much of a struggle. My mother and father hadn't painted a happy picture of family life for us.

However, once David and I were settled in our little stone cottage in the suburbs, I felt more secure and well-loved than I had in my entire life. In his thirties and keen to have a child with me, he managed to talk me into this reckless scheme, which I agreed to without seriously thinking through the many implications. I just wanted to make him happy. Perhaps he believed that if we had a child together it would further cement our relationship.

It took nearly a year, but eventually I conceived and I couldn't believe how delighted we both felt. I was floating on air for months and as my body changed shape David seemed to love me even more. In those days we didn't wear gorgeous tight-fitting maternity clothes like young pregnant women do today – we wore loose-fitting tent dresses intended to disguise our expanding bellies. But I was proud of my expanding body shape and I felt so healthy, so energetic and quite beautiful. I worked all the way through, right up until the day before the birth.

David wasn't with me to see our daughter, Miriam, born after an uncomplicated labour. The era of fathers being at the birth hadn't yet arrived and David chose the 'I won't be able to cope' option. I must have been a remarkably resilient and determined young woman to manage alone at such a tender age. The midwives were wonderful, of course, and I felt so empowered that I rose to the occasion.

I believe this is when I properly fell in love with David. Holding our child in my arms sealed a bond that continued over the next four decades. Hormones play a huge part in the crazy love that envelops new mothers and this adoration made me view David through different eyes.

Luckily I took to motherhood with comparative ease. I was exhausted by constant sleep interruption but Miriam settled into a routine quickly and I adjusted to stumbling around in the middle of the night to feed my sweet, tiny baby. She made me smile constantly.

This newborn bliss didn't last as long as I hoped. I'd more or less resigned from my job on the television magazine, expecting to be an at-home mum for at least twelve months, but Miriam was barely five weeks old when David arrived home with a face like thunder and the devastating news that his new family television show *The People Next Door* had been axed by the channel. We had no savings and a new mortgage to pay, so several weeks later I weaned little Miriam and went back to my old job. It was a heartbreaking necessity but the saving grace was that a close friend who lived nearby with her husband and two pre-school children offered to care for Miriam five days a week. We paid her the going rate, of course, but it was such a casual arrangement compared to childcare options and regulations these days. Somehow it worked.

By the time I was pregnant with our son Aaron, David had found work in the film industry and I no longer needed to work such long hours. But I did continue working part-time while juggling two young children for several years, and I also stayed at home for a period to became a day-care mother with extra children to care for, including little Tony, whose mother had returned to work fulltime. I loved children and I adored being a mother, even though it was hard work. The fun aspects of having kids around far outweighed the drudgery.

During this stage of my life, in the mid-seventies, I began reading about the use of chemicals in agriculture that eventually ended up in the food chain. From my research I realised that the fruit and vegetables that landed on my kitchen bench had probably been treated with chemicals – pesticides, fungicides, and artificial fertilisers. I didn't want this for my children and I embraced the organic gardening and farming movement. I'd become a bit of a hippie, an evolution that David observed with some amusement. But after all, I was a product of the rebellious 1960s: I'd marched and demonstrated against nuclear armaments, the Vietnam War and the treatment of Indigenous Australians.

When I get a notion in my head it's hard to shake it. Poor David. His work was Sydney-based but I was suddenly determined that the family should move away from the urban smog and traffic up to the cool fresh ridges of the Blue Mountains where I could find land and start growing our food. We had also acquired an additional family member. By his early sixties, my father was raddled by smoking, alcoholism and a multitude of physical ailments. He ended his own life with a bottle of whisky and thirty sleeping tablets. Shattered, my mother, Muriel, came to live with us in our tiny home – at first it was a temporary arrangement but she travelled with us to the mountains and remained part of our household until she died more than twenty-five years later.

In Leura we found the perfect old weatherboard house surrounded by enough cleared land to start my gardening project. By force of sheer enthusiasm and determination I carved a large orchard and vegetable patch from the sandy, barren soil using manure and mushroom compost and set up runs and shelters for chickens and ducks. I knew nothing about gardening so borrowed books from the library and subscribed to gardening magazines. My neighbour had an amazing ornamental garden and we chatted over the fence continuously. She was quick to point out when I was doing something wrong. Hit and miss; trial and error: I learned to garden the hard way.

Once we were living in Leura, David camped in his city office Monday to Friday and joined the family fray only at the weekends. In some ways this suited me because I could get on with the busyness of my life without interruption during the week and then welcome him with open arms on Friday nights. Having a part-time husband added frisson. I would wait for him in bed as he often didn't leave the city until late. We would stay in bed as long as possible on Saturday and Sunday mornings while my mother supervised the children's breakfast. Following my family's tradition I always cooked a big Sunday lunch and afterwards we would all go for a long rambling bushwalk, often down the track to Wentworth Falls.

Two years after moving to the mountains David's son, Tony, came to live with us – by then he was seven years old. It was a swap – he spent the weekdays with us, going to the same school as his half siblings, and every second weekend with his mother in Sydney. Then a year after this adjustment I realised that I was expecting another child. David was a little overwhelmed. He hadn't anticipated such a big family but he steadily warmed to the idea and Ethan was born at home with the entire family dancing around our bedroom with joy. Now we had a large and noisy extended family of three generations. Three adults and four children, plus numerous pets and poultry. I was in my element.

My career suffered a blow when we moved from the city. In the era before computers it was hard to find work as a freelance writer unless you were on the spot and very few journalists were able to work from home, especially when living far from the city. But although my desire to be an organic gardener caused a hiccup in my career path, over time it opened up a whole new and exciting direction. From being a showbusiness reporter I became a gardening writer. There were no blogs in 1976 so I started tentatively writing about my dalliance with horticulture in a column for the magazine *Home Journal*. The readers found it refreshing to be given encouraging gardening advice that was accessible, focusing on the joys and benefits of turning the soil. There was nothing dry or scientific in my prose. Through a publishing contact of David's, I was contracted to write a book which I called *The Good Life*. It chronicled our flight from the city and the way in which we had embraced semi-rural self-sufficiency, with chapters on keeping chickens, cooking on a wood stove and growing vegetables and herbs. It was a wonderful opportunity for me to champion my love of this lifestyle and in many respects launched my new career path.

Before long I was approached to put my journalistic skills to work in the editing and production of various gardening books and magazines. I worked on an electric typewriter and a small fortune was spent on couriers running manuscripts and photographs back and forth from Sydney to Leura. It was a perfect pathway, allowing me to be a stay-at-home mum with the support of my own mother while earning a good income at a desk in the corner of our bedroom.

Eventually my books and magazine column were noticed by the producers of the ABC's popular weekly TV show, *Gardening Australia*. I auditioned and became a regular member of the team in 1991. It was a heady and hectic ten years of researching, writing scripts and filming, as well as contributing articles and photographs to the monthly magazine. I kept up my freelance writing as well, as the author or editor of at least two glossy books every year. It was my busiest decade. I had finally found my specialisation and was delighted that my passion had become my career.

My decade on *Gardening Australia* was undoubtedly the most hectic and exciting period of my working life. The popular weekly show was produced from the Hobart studios of the ABC because the star of the program, the irrepressible Peter Cundall, was based in Launceston. There was a presenter appointed for every state and I was given the job of covering all things horticultural in NSW, from the north coast to the western plains. Once a month a small film crew of cameraman, sound recordist and producer would fly to the mainland to spend four or five days filming seven- or eight-minute segments with each of us in rotation.

This small team set a very high production standard. We would spend an entire day – up to nine hours without a break – recording just one of these short segments which then had to be edited together when they returned to Tasmania. Every show had a balance of different stories from each state – something practical, something pretty, an interview with a successful gardener or a trip to one of our many botanic gardens.

We did vegetables, flowers, fruit, herbs, water gardens and lawns – showed viewers how to lay paths and build walls and pergolas. I often filmed in my own garden in Leura because I had such a mix of different 'scenes' from a deep back verandah decorated with pots and hanging baskets to a shady fernery, a wide vegetable garden with herbs, seasonal vegetables and fruits interplanted with flowering annuals, a small birch woodland and a sunny area densely planted with old-fashioned roses and perennials. It was like a mini film set and we would get the kettle boiling in the kitchen then set up our recording gear and spend many happy days creating segments that were both practical and entertaining. It was tremendous fun. I loved introducing people to the show and I tracked down elderly gardeners (most over eighty-five who still worked in their gardens most days); eccentric experts on specific subjects such as molluscs (snails) and fungi and obsessive blokes who laboured half the year growing 'perfect' dahlias for competition in their local flower shows. These characters added such richness to the mix and I believe their contribution set our show apart from other similar programs.

In between visits from the film crew I spent a lot of time researching new ideas and topics, looking for suitable locations and finding new and fascinating people to interview. I was also writing articles for the monthly glossy *Gardening Australia* magazine and taking lots and lots of photographs of plants and gardens that we were featuring on the show. I also continued writing and editing books and magazines for other publishers and often worked well into the night, after dinner when the house was finally quiet. I was constantly on the go because during this decade I also had four teenage children at various stages of their education and my mother had started becoming frail and less able to take over from me if I was required to travel as part of my work. It wasn't lost on me that my earlier ambition to be a television reporter had finally been realised, although not quite in the way I'd anticipated. Instead of reporting from the steps of Parliament House I was filing stories from botanical gardens and the backyards of everyday suburban garden enthusiasts. I loved my job and the people I met, from the experts to the amateurs, and all my colleagues. I was in my forties and enjoying 'the good life' in every way. I also enjoyed all the spin-offs from doing the TV show, including writing and editing books and magazines, doing gardening talkback radio programs and becoming a popular guest speaker at gardening clubs and groups around Australia. I was also regularly leading botanical treks and tours in China and the Indian Himalayas and working diligently in my own large garden, which I sometimes opened to the public.

During this phase of our lives David was equally engaged in his work, travelling internationally with films being produced in Scotland, New York, the Philippines and New Zealand. We sometimes wouldn't see each other for months at a time and in those days overseas communication was much more difficult and expensive. It wasn't in any sense a conventional marriage but when we did find moments to spend together, especially with the children, it was our 'precious' time.

Then, in my late forties, our family life changed considerably. Gradually our children had grown up and left home to further their education – Tony to Sydney, Miriam to Canberra, and Ethan and Aaron moving to northern Lismore where they studied horticulture. It amused me that any of our children would follow me into gardening as a career – I imagined they'd find their father's work in the film industry much more glamorous and exciting. Both Miriam and Aaron were in serious relationships and between them had three children in their early twenties. I was now, to my surprise, a (very young) grandmother. Then my mother suddenly died, leaving a huge void in all our lives. My world seemed very different.

4

The clinic

David has a particular type of malignancy called an adeno-carcinoma, which we're told is the culmination of many years of gastric reflux eroding the tissue where the oesophagus joins the stomach. After the scan in Sydney, when we were advised the condition was inoperable, we were given referrals to two oncology specialists – one for radiation and one for chemotherapy.

I have always known that some specialists, amazing and knowledgeable as they are, can be narrow or blinkered in their focus. Some may only see the problem – such as the tumour – and not the human being as a whole. I remember decades ago a friend who, shortly after giving birth, was diagnosed with an aggressive brain tumour. The brain surgeon offered plenty of information and advice, but when my friend asked if she could continue lactating after the surgery and during the treatment, he was totally nonplussed. 'What's lactating?' he asked. He knew just about everything there was to know about a brain, but nothing whatsoever about a mother's breasts.

The radiation oncologist is the first specialist we meet. He lacks warmth.

'What have you been told?' the specialist asks David.

'That the tumour is inoperable,' David responds glumly.

'Yes,' he concurs. 'Inoperable, incurable and terminal.'

Well, he's definitely not mincing his words! A social worker is sitting in on the consultation and I wonder if she's required for additional support if people respond negatively to his apparent complete lack of compassion.

Rubbing salt into the wound, he asks David to remove his shirt and sit on a low stool. Standing behind him, the specialist palpates under David's left collar bone then invites me to come over and also dig my fingertips in behind the bone to feel the tumour that is part of the metastasis. I can indeed feel a hard lump. I wish I'd refused to do it.

Even though he still doesn't really believe the bad news, David asks the inevitable: 'How long do I have?'

'It could be a matter of six months or it could be as long as eighteen months,' the doctor says. 'The average is a year.'

'And what will actually kill me?'

'Starvation probably. The tumour will block the entrance to the stomach. We can put in a valve and feed you directly into the stomach,' he adds, as if we'll be thrilled at this prospect.

'No way will I be doing that!' David fires back.

And no way will David ever starve to death, I think to myself.

I recall almost nothing from the rest of this dismal appointment. Dr Death, as David quickly nicknames him, lists a few radiotherapy centres for us to consider – some in Sydney and some in the bush. David opts for the rural centre of Wagga Wagga, about four hours' drive from our home, as he doesn't fancy spending a whole month in the city. Also, knowing I'll be away leading a trek for the first seven days of the treatment, he is consoled that Lilier Lodge, a large country town facility, has comfortable patient accommodation funded by two cancer-support organisations – a combination of government funding and, once again, community fundraising.

There's also the issue of our finances. Although we've paid for basic medical insurance for decades, David is reluctant to use it because the gap payment can be alarming. As self-employed people working in the arts we don't have superannuation – we own our small farm and have some modest savings. David has always handled the money side of things in our relationship, and he's a worrier by nature. He rarely, if ever, spends any money on himself – I have to drag him under protest to replace jackets and trousers that are worn at the knees and elbows, and I'm grudgingly allowed to replace socks and jocks only when they become threadbare. It follows that if being treated in the bush is a cheaper option that's always going to be the one he will choose. For me, I just want him to have the best possible treatment;

the best chance of survival. It will, in time, become a sticking point between us.

We have a numb, dazed drive back to the farm. I had a strong gut instinct to be with David on every step of this frightening journey. Imagine having a session like that one, with Dr Death, all on your own. Having an ally during medical meetings is essential. David doesn't necessarily remember everything that has been discussed or, rather, he chooses to remember only what he wants to hear. He rarely thinks of the right questions to ask at the time and never challenges a course of action that is proposed, which is just not like him at all.

It's chilly enough to light the fire in the sitting room when we get home. I put a pot of soup on the fuel stove and pour us each a stiff gin and tonic. We need to deconstruct the last hour.

This dying situation has galvanised us like never before. In more than forty years together we've spent plenty of time apart – David virtually lived in his Sydney office Monday to Friday for more than twenty years and was always away for several months at a time when a film was in production. We had done several fantastic overseas trips together, but when the children were grown I started travelling without him, as a tour guide, so we had developed very independent and self-sufficient lives. Yet we were singularly intertwined emotionally, and I know we'll need to depend on each other during the weeks, months and hopefully years ahead.

That afternoon, during a long lunch with wine, we discuss the effects of negativity on people who are sick. From my perspective, while I understand the need for the radiation oncologist to be clear and frank – to be certain that we understand both the diagnosis and prognosis – I believe his brutal manner was counterproductive. Demoralising. Discouraging. Dispiriting.

David, on the other hand, just really wants to kill him. He's a fighter and not known for taking shit from people. The medico–patient relationship can be a tough one to handle – from both sides. I'm amused David has come up with the nickname Dr Death for this chap. In a way it's stiffened our resolve to combat this medical skepticism, and from my perspective anything that brings humour into a situation has to be a positive.

We also talk about the next tour I'm set to lead, which will coincide with the first seven days of David's radiotherapy treatment. I really don't want to go ahead with it but David is absolutely adamant. David's stubborn insistence that I continue to work is no doubt because he's thinking ahead, knowing I'll need to survive financially after he's no longer around. I do understand, too, that he needs life to feel as 'normal' as possible, but I fear I'll be anxious the entire time knowing what he's enduring while I'm climbing up some mountainside in Sikkim. It would be difficult to back out because the trip is fully booked and organised down to the last sleeping bag, yet how can I comfortably leave him to deal with this medical situation alone?

5

Finding my feet

1994 AND BEYOND

David was all in favour of my treks from the start. It was thanks to *Gardening Australia* that I found myself branching into a completely unexpected second career as a tour guide in 1994. Many of my weekly segments were about cool climate plants because of our location up in the mountains. The adventure travel company World Expeditions knew a large percentage of their trekkers were over forty – some even well into their fifties, sixties and seventies. These adventurous older people were captivated by the beauty of the flora, especially on Himalayan treks in India, China, Nepal and Bhutan. The local guides generally could only provide the common names of these plants so the tour company decided to establish a series of botanical treks in different regions of the Himalayas, using well-known

Australian gardening writers and television presenters as tour escorts.

I was one of those approached and it caught me a little off guard. I'd never contemplated trekking although I'd previously led a few groups on overseas garden tours – which were all about taking busloads of people to visit famous gardens while staying in comfortable hotels. I'd only even been camping twice in my life and wasn't sure I'd enjoy roughing it.

David, as usual, had championed the idea, encouraging me to jump in feet first. He saw it as a great opportunity and because my mother was there to care for the children he could see no reason for me not to go. Neither of us suspected that first Himalayan trek would be a life-changing experience.

My first trek was to the Indian Himalayas, and the itinerary was exotic and exciting. I was to meet my group in New Delhi where I would also be introduced to our local guide. I arrived with all the paraphernalia of a professional trekker, rather nervous and desperately hoping to look the part. I had stylish new khaki hiking pants with a matching long-sleeved shirt, a fancy new backpack and wildly expensive Italian leather hiking boots. Outwardly I was trying to be confident yet mentally I was completely unprepared for what lay ahead.

From Delhi we caught an early morning train heading towards the university city of Dehra Dun in the foothills of the Himalayas. Stepping over the sleeping homeless families curled up on the railway platform before sunrise was a culture shock. I grabbed the hand of one woman in our group who was quite shaken at the experience. She later told me that this was her first overseas trip – she had arrived after dark the previous evening and the early morning introduction to the real India was a little overwhelming.

On the train we gathered ourselves and began getting to know each other while our local guide organised a hearty breakfast for us, along with endless cups of steaming hot tea. The five-hour journey was a revelation as we sped past poor villages and fields being worked with animals and primitive implements, and old men crouching by the railway line just watching the trains rattle past or sleeping under a tree on a simple timber-framed bed. The squat toilets on the train were a bit of a challenge but everyone coped with good humour and stoicism.

In Dehra Dun we visited the university and met our tour botanist, an elegant and gently spoken man whose life's work was the flora of the valley we would be trekking through. Next we set off in four-wheel drive vehicles up a steep and winding road with perpendicular cliffs on one side and a terrifyingly steep drop to the valley floor on the other. Our destination was the former British hill station of Mussoorie.

I was astonished to see so many familiar trees and shrubs lining the roadside – eucalyptus, callistemon, acacias and jacarandas. Our botanist explained that during the era of the British Raj, plants were introduced from other colonies. I'm quite certain most of them must have become environmental threats, just as many introduced plants are in Australia. It was weird to see nodding heads of native Australian bottle-brush and wattle in such an alien setting.

Mussoorie is a bustling and beautiful town at an altitude just over 2000 metres with spectacular views to the surrounding mountains. This was my first real up close and personal encounter with the Himalayas and I was immediately smitten. The view from my hotel window brought tears to my eyes. They weren't the last tears I would shed over the next two weeks.

Even though the trip notes from the travel company advised us that the walking level was 'intermediate' I romantically visualised myself skipping through meadows of glorious wild-flowers without fully appreciating that to reach a lush alpine meadow at an altitude of more than 3500 metres necessitated thousands and thousands (and thousands) of trudging steps up steep and slippery tracks, slithering over assorted splatters of animal dung. Still in my early forties, I assumed I had a natural fitness and I was soon humbled to acknowledge that many of my older charges were more experienced and fitter walkers than me. My feet were so blistered from my no-longer-shiny new shoes that on day two I walked barefoot over rocks rather than endure any further agony. In every sense it was a steep learning curve.

Our destination was the cradle-shaped Har Ki Dun plateau, which is generally described as a hanging valley because it appears suspended within the powerful snow-covered peaks of the Garhwal Himalayas. We set out from a small village called Taluka and were fascinated by the traditional way of life and the nomadic Gujar shepherds who have been tending their flocks here since the sixth century. The shepherds have their own language and variously practise Hinduism, Sikhism and Islam. They live in portable shelters and the entire family travels together with the herds during the summer season. We walked alongside vast flocks of goats, sheep and domesticated buffalo and wobbled across rickety bridges that need to be rebuilt every summer, after being washed away by the early spring melting snows.

I was thrilled by the richness of this valley. Watered by melting snow, the alpine meadows are a lush and brilliant green, creating a panorama against the massive snow-topped mountains backed by a clear blue sky. We had ascended above the dense mixed forests of pine, spruce and fir into open grasslands with icy streams edged with swathes of marsh marigolds and buttercups. We were surrounded by waxflowers, edelweiss, primulas, iris, daphne and gentians. These flowering perennials and alpine shrubs were not just in clumps, but stretched as far as the eye could see. We camped for two nights in this paradise recovering from the six days of uphill slog, the bleeding feet and aching calves (well that's just me). I sat on the edge of a freezing cold stream and soaked my unhappy feet until they turned blue.

Here I had time to work with the botanist and properly identify many of the plants we'd been admiring along the way. In my backpack I was lugging two huge botanical text-books and a heavy bag of camera equipment – multiple lenses and lots of film. It was back in the days of photographic slides and projectors. I had been researching the botanical history of the Himalayas and discovered that these glorious mountains provided one of the richest diversity of plants in the world. During the ice ages, when the western plains of Europe were ravaged by ice and frost, the mountains were protected by a thick smothering of snow that allowed more than 25,000 species to survive.

So many of the plants we love in our gardens – perennials, roses, bulbs, shrubs and trees – are from this very region. Over the last three centuries they were gathered – some would say stolen – by botanical explorers, romantically known as plant hunters, who pillaged the foothills and alpine valleys of their riches. These then came into cultivation via institutions such as the British Kew Gardens and the collections of the French aristocracy. All this detail combined with the knowl-edge of our local botanist and guides added so much to the entire experience.

Although the walking was tough at times, we were well supported by the local team of cooks, guide and porters. To my amazement most of the gear – the tents, the cooking equipment and our sleeping bags and clothes – were carried by people, not animals. In later treks, pack animals such as ponies, camels, donkeys and dzoes (a cross between a yak and a cow) were used in different regions. I was astonished at the strength and resilience of the mountain people who made the trek possible.

There was no electricity up here, no satellite or possibility of a phone connection. It was the isolation and the extreme beauty of our surroundings that really got to me. Although I was physically tired from the exertion of the daily trekking, I was emotionally wired from finding myself in such a remarkable place. I really had to push myself to reach this destination, and it was worth every step. I loved the absolute silence in our tents at night, being so far removed from civilisation. During the day I was often moved beyond words by what I saw: the small villages we walked through, the children running to greet us, the older women smiling shyly, the way of life I would never have seen if I hadn't joined this adventure. All my senses were heightened; I was elated by it all, and I knew I could never have felt this sensation without determination and an open heart.

One afternoon we were nearing our welcoming campsite when I wandered around a huge boulder on the side of the hill and found myself surrounded by a sea of nodding *Fritillaria meleagris*. For years I had struggled to grow these fussy members of the lily family without much success. Fritillaries can be quite tricky plants in cultivation yet here I was, knee-deep in a meadow of them, drifting down the hillside in a profusion of deep purple and white patterned petals. The tears poured down my cheeks. This is why I came, I thought; to be deeply touched by the scale of everything around me. The rest of the group gathered to share the moment, bonded in beauty.

Back in Sydney to debrief with World Expeditions, I was high as a kite on the thrill of our journey and could barely find the words to describe how much I had gained from this opportunity. I just couldn't stop smiling, knowing that for me, walking deep into the mountains had been profound. The sense of exhilaration and achievement I felt! I was completely hooked.

Since that first extraordinary trek, over two more decades I was to accompany groups every year – sometimes two or three times a year – to many different parts of the world. From up-market European and English garden tours to cultural and botanical trips in western China, Bhutan, Kashmir and other regions of India, including Darjeeling and Sikkim, as well as historic Nepal at the foot of Mount Everest. It gave my life a powerful, deep dimension. Seeing first hand and experiencing the life of people in remote regions altered my understanding of the world. It gave me a new perspective on my own life and the privileges I had taken for granted. Once I had the opportunity to take two of my teenage grandsons trekking in Nepal and that was also a life-changing experience for them. I am fortunate indeed that my fascination with plants has opened so many doors and given me a life more exciting and enriching than I could ever have imagined.

6

leaving David behind

WAGGA, APRIL 2012

David won the battle so I will be leaving him for just over two weeks and honouring my commitment to the Indian trek. We decide to drive to Wagga and check out the radiation clinic and Lilier Lodge, the guest facility where he will be staying. It will ease my mind to have a mental picture of where David will be staying while I'm away. We make a mini-holiday of it, being on the road for three days just a week before I'm due to fly to India. We stay overnight in a motel, have a country town dinner, explore the countryside and enjoy some precious time together. I suddenly recall the name of a woman from this region who came on one of my China trips more than twenty years ago. She was a marvellous soul, full of life and fun, and I decide to contact her and see if she can spend some time with David during that first seven days when he's alone – before I'm able to join him.

Then all too soon I'm on the early morning flight to Kolkata, the capital of West Bengal, and feeling anxious because for the first time I just don't seem mentally or physically prepared to meet the eager trekking group that will arrive over the next two days. I'm fretting about David, worrying how his body and, more importantly, his mind, will be coping with the assault of radiation.

For those who love India, as I do, it's thrilling to step off a bus or a train or a jeep onto the main street of Darjeeling and realise you have time-travelled back to the era of the British Raj: the colonial hill station architecture; the sprawling, grand old hotels that serve high tea every afternoon; the Christian church spires and British-style boarding schools that still thrive – these days filled with aspirational students from Kolkata and Delhi. Darjeeling has a turbulent history and a fascinating mix of people and cultures from the surrounding regions of Nepal, Bhutan, Sikkim and the plains of Bengal.

It's a well-preserved reminder of what is promoted as a 'romantic' past but in truth was a maelstrom of upheavals, uprisings, and political and economic power struggles. The tension continues to this day as the militant Gorkha movement agitates for autonomy.

At an attitude of 2100 metres, it was the temperate climate and pleasing views of the mountains that first convinced the British to create a summer escape from the hellish heat of

Calcutta, as Kolkata was then called. Our charming hotel – the Cedar Inn – is very Raj-style with gabled dormers decorated with ornate trims. On arrival we're served fine china cups of local tea before being taken to our spacious rooms, each with an open fireplace for winter guests. The hotel has fantastic views but that comes with a steep walk up and down from the main shopping street. If the mist lifts, it reveals the world's third-highest mountain, Kangchenjunga, in all its glory. It will take a day or two to acclimatise before the next stage – the trek into Sikkim – so we spend our time walking from one end of the township to the other. Many of the buildings are slightly decayed but this only adds to the charm. There's a gymkhana club, a district library crammed with ancient tomes, several traditional churches and cemeteries with names like St Andrew's and St Paul's, a Loreto College, a posh Tea Planter's Club and a UNESCO-listed railway station. All cheek by jowl with Buddhist monasteries, Hindu temples, a Tibetan refugee centre and the Himalayan Mountaineering Institute where all the guides for our various adventures have been trained.

The British left India in 1947 when Partition ended Crown rule but a few brave souls remained in Darjeeling and many other parts of the country with their families – the children who were born here wouldn't have known any other life. Every so often I catch a glimpse of an elderly, neatly dressed Englishwoman – eighty-five years plus – out and about shopping, laughing and chatting with the locals, and walking slowly up and down all these steep streets without footpaths. In a local bookshop I discover a delightfully well-written account of these remnants of the period, complete with photographs of dignified men and women, some obviously now living in genteel poverty, sipping tea and talking about their lives in this faraway corner of the world. I completely understand why they decided to stay. It's such a captivating place, and for those born in India, being outcasts sent to live in England would have been anathema.

Then there are the tea plantations. As a tea lover I have mixed feelings about the picture-perfect rolling landscape of hillsides smothered with neatly clipped *Camellia sinensis* tended by teams of local women colourfully dressed in saris. It's pleasing to the eye, but the underlying story reflects the downside of colonialisation. As the species name (*sinensis*) suggests, the original tea plant was smuggled out of China by plant hunters and controversially introduced to India in the 1830s as a hugely profitable agricultural crop. The history of the British and plant exploration or exploitation, whichever way you like to look at it, is politically and ethically not a palatable one. Although the tea plantations of Darjeeling are vital to the regional economy, the conditions for the women who tend and harvest the crops are far from ideal. They rise very early to pluck leaf tips before the heat of the day, then return to the fields again in the evening. Their wages are meagre considering the retail price of the product.

Our local guides take us through an extraordinary and cavernous old tea processing factory, where the freshly plucked leaf tips are half-dried, rolled, fermented, sorted, graded and then packaged. I'm not a coffee drinker – never have been – so here I'm in a tea lover's paradise. I buy packets and packets of variously graded leaves to take home, both as gifts and to enjoy drinking myself. Darjeeling tea is sublime; possibly the best in the world. At the Cedar Inn you can order early morning bed tea – my most treasured indulgence. At 6.30 am a man arrives (I leave the door unlocked) with a silver tray and teapot, a fine china cup and saucer and one plain digestive biscuit. I'm still warmly tucked up as he places the tray at the foot of my bed and sweetly pours the fragrant tea. I can't imagine a more blissful way to start the day and it reminds me of how things are at home, with David bringing me tea in bed every morning.

This is a different group from my typical botanical treks. Yoga is the focus, and that brings a distinctive group dynamic – mostly women of a certain age who like adventure and love yoga. They are relishing Darjeeling, but after two days we get organised and head up to Sikkim, home of the nature-loving Lepchas. Sikkim was once a kingdom and it, too, was affected by British colonisation, becoming a protectorate. We have to hand over our passports and be issued with visas before entering the ornate gateway that marks the beginning of our journey into the mountains.

We are met by our trekking crew – cooks, porters, guides and the horsemen who wrangle the ponies that will carry our gear. It's all very civilised, really. We carry light daypacks – just an emergency raincoat, hat, sunscreen, water, camera. The porters and cooks go ahead with the tents, the food and our luggage so by the time we've huffed and puffed up the side of the mountain our tents are up, the kettle is boiled for tea and the ponies are grazing all around us. The trek is from the village of Yuksam to Dzongri, which is just over 4000 metres above sea level. The views are sublime, and we pass hillsides of dwarf rhododendrons and delightful villages where the local children rush out to greet us.

Although trekking can be tough at times, there is unquestionably a meditative aspect to the rhythm of our walking. Time for talking, too, as we gradually ascend, and also to stop and take photographs and soak up the beauty around us. We are a small group of eight, which makes it possible to bond with everyone along the way. At various times I walk alongside and talk with each person, sharing some of my funny and encouraging anecdotes from previous treks. I have an oft-repeated mantra: 'Trekking is more in your head than in your legs'. At the beginning of every trek a few individuals can be daunted at the prospect of lengthy walks uphill at altitude, and this expresses itself in a fear of 'holding everyone up' or 'slowing down the pace'. In groups, people always walk at differing paces and I'm happy if we spread out a little – each mini group with a guide nearby. These treks should never be seen as a race or a competition. It's an experience to be savoured, not a gruelling ordeal to be endured. If you walk too fast you miss the scenery along the way, all the small things like birds and miniature alpine plants. This trip has the added bonus of two yoga sessions a day; the first before breakfast to loosen our limbs for the walk ahead; the second after we have wound down a little, and before the evening meal is served. Sunrise and sunset. It's deeply satisfying for all involved. Everyone makes it to camp each day and I love the expressions on the faces when we first catch sight of those orange tents in the distance.

I get to know one delightful woman from Melbourne who lost her comparatively young husband to cancer several years before. I confide in her, describing my fears for David. Her insights into that period between diagnosis and death are fascinating to me, and her pragmatic empathy is a great comfort. She and her husband had such a different journey. They went to seminars and workshops on death and dying and they tried a range of alternative treatments and manage-ment regimes. They had counselling and did meditation. It seems to me that all David and I are doing is avoiding any discussion of what lies ahead. Oh, and having afternoon naps. It's comforting to know that I'm not alone in this harrowing reality and I'm grateful to be living at a time when we can discuss death and dying more openly, and share knowledge and ideas. When I was growing up in the 1950s, cancer was such a terrifying concept nobody ever spoke about it. People who were sick and dying of cancer were hidden from sight and only mentioned after they had politely died.

I'm glad I went on this trek. Even though it has taken me away from David during a critical time of his treatment, it's given me some much-needed thinking time, a little distance and a lot of strength.

I don't carry a lot of technology when I travel, especially on treks to remote places. I have an old Australian mobile which I switch off most of the time, and I don't want the hassle of carrying a laptop. Back in Darjeeling after the trek, I ask the hotel for access to a computer so I can send an email to David. When we visited Wagga where he is having the radiation he sussed out an excellent local library which had a well equipped computer room. He planned to drop in once or twice a day to keep in touch with our children and his wide circle of film industry friends. Like a lot of blokes in his age group, David was slow to embrace technology, but once he got the hang of sending and receiving emails and playing around with Google, there was no stopping him. He's definitely an obsessive, so I know he will have been spending hours and hours every day at the library.

In my email I describe Darjeeling and the trek in Sikkim in some detail – the people and the scenery with a few amusing anecdotes, such as the herd of goats who chewed our wet washing draped over the bushes in the late afternoon sun, thrown in for fun. Several hours later I check for a return email and, sure enough, there's a long, newsy letter from him. He seems in great spirits, saying the place he's staying is marvellous and that he's bonded with the other patients and also spent lots of time with my old tour buddy, Olga, who he describes as 'an absolute gem'. She has cooked him soups and baked cakes, and they go out for coffee every day. I breathe a sigh of relief because he hasn't slumped into melancholia, although I'm still very anxious to get back to Sydney and catch the flight down to Wagga to join him.

I see him standing behind the fence at the small country airport to meet me, grinning ear to ear. How many times has he come to pick me up after a trek, waving from the safety barrier? We hug; a long, hard hug. The patient accommodation at the clinic is attractive, comfortable and homely. We have a large en suite bedroom with an outdoor sitting area, television and small dining table if we decide to eat alone, a huge communal sitting room with television and a well-stocked library. There's also a kitchen large enough for four or five people to cook at the same time and a long, shared dining room table. We go shopping and I start cooking – all his favourite soups and stews and baked custards.

A bus picks us up every morning to transfer us to the radiation clinic. The drivers are volunteers – cheery older retired blokes mostly – who personalise this service with humour. The procedure is speedy with virtually no waiting time. I'm beginning to think that David's decision to opt for rural rather than big-city care is an intelligent one. It's friendlier and more personal. I wonder if patients and their carers feel lost in a big city hospital or clinic.

The next two weeks are spent enjoying country life, although David is starting to feel the acute effects of the radiation. We were warned that radiation would stir things up – agitate the tumour – so we were mentally prepared. David finds it increasingly hard to swallow food and Dr Death's prediction of starvation haunts me. I make softer food – what my Mum would have called invalid food in the old days – but loaded with flavour. His tastebuds are still working and he enjoys his strong coffee, his creamy soups and the odd gin and tonic. I get to know some of his new friends. It's a strangely convivial time.

Driving back to the farm after the treatment's ended, we don't rush, meandering and enjoying pretty country towns where we stop for food, coffee or beer along the way. Now at home we face the reality of the months ahead – the chemotherapy. This is described as the most traumatic stage of cancer treatment as the drugs take a huge toll on the human body while they are attacking the malignant cells. I'm not sure about David, but I'm dreading the prospect of seeing him suffer through this.

By the time he's due to start the eight rounds of chemotherapy, there's no longer a permanent specialist visiting rural Bathurst so we've been referred to one in Sydney.

Our response to meeting this doctor is a revelation – we instantly feel confident with him and his treatment approach. He is honest and practical, yet offers hope of a decent quality of life, and encouragement like this is essential for us at this critical time, both mentally and physically.

David establishes an immediate rapport with him and his upbeat approach – he couldn't be more different from Dr Death.

Among many things, our new doctor gives us advice about the toxicity of the drugs being used, pointing out the dangers of my coming in contact with any of David's body fluids – saliva, blood, urine or semen. In a roundabout way he is warning us that, as David's carer and wife, I need to be cautious about any intimate contact. It's obvious that for six months sex will be completely out of the question. I expect he is more accustomed to giving this sort of advice to much younger patients and their partners but he is covering all the bases. It gives us pause for thought.

While in Sydney we visit our newest grandchild – our tenth – a precious little girl named Alena who is the firstborn of David's son Tony and his wife, Leslie. She's exquisite, just a few days old and I'm struck by the importance of this new generation in helping us to come to terms with what we are going through. David hasn't reached that stage yet, of appreciating the importance of being able to let go and hand on to our children and grandchildren. This new life touches me deeply, reassuring me that what we are facing is simply what nature intends. That we are just part of the normal cycle of life, and that death is just one more step in this cycle.

It's all very well and good for me to think this way – I'm not the one with cancer cells bouncing around and destroying my body.

7

Country life

Living on a farm was always a fantasy for me, probably stemming from the wonderful holiday times I spent at the properties of family friends as a child. I have always loved the feeling of space, the paddocks and trees, the animals and the smell of the shearing shed. Of not being able to see another house or driveway. I would've loved a farm when our own children were little, somewhere that would give them the freedom to run wild and be in contact with nature and animals. The Leura house was a pretty good compromise, with enough space to create a mini-farm with chickens and ducks, fruit trees and a huge vegetable garden.

The village of Leura, where we had lived for twenty-six years, had changed dramatically during that time. The irony is not lost on me that it was mass tourism that made us decide to leave and settle at a farm at Yetholme, thirty kilometres east of Bathurst. I was thrilled at the prospect of offering our grandchildren the opportunity to experience the fun and freedom I'd enjoyed as a kid. Miriam, her husband and their four sons were living in Bathurst by then, so the move was partly motivated by a desire to be closer to them. David no longer needed to have a city office as most of his business was conducted via phone and internet, making it possible for him to work from home.

Initially it was the big old farmhouse and not the land that attracted me. Set at the top of a gentle slope down to the creek, the house was built in the 1920s of locally kilned red brick with a tin roof and wide verandas at the back and front which are wonderful in summer. The winters at Yetholme are long and hard and the design of the house is perfect for staying warm because the rooms are comparatively small, with high ceilings. There are five fireplaces, three of which I keep going most days in autumn and winter – in the kitchen, the family room and our bedroom. We have plenty of wood scattered around the farm and our sons are always willing to cut up dead trees for use in the house. There's a formal sitting and dining room; the old maid's quarters which became a family room, and a spacious kitchen also with a dining area plus a massive walk-in pantry. There are five large bedrooms as well as a glassed-in veranda which makes a perfect office for me, with pretty views of the garden.

The house was built by a local couple who made a small fortune on the goldfields of Western Australia. After they died, for two decades it was a residential home for adults with disabilities and housed sixteen people comfortably, including their carers. It's certainly big enough for our ever-expanding family and the large original Yetholme community dance hall tucked away behind the house is a great place for kids to play when the weather is bad, or for big family parties.

At twenty-five acres, the property was never really going to be a viable working farm, although at one stage we did invest in some propagation greenhouses with the thought of setting up a small native nursery. We soon discovered that we wouldn't have enough water to make this a going concern as the natural spring from which we pumped water for the house and garden dropped dramatically during several years of drought. At one point we needed to buy in water by the tanker load just to keep the house and vegetable garden going.

When we first arrived we had a small ride-on mower which we quickly realised was not up to the task of keeping the pasture down over such a massive area. The decision was taken to fence off large areas on both sides of the house and create paddocks for grazing animals. Initially we had some of our neighbour's cattle on agistment, but in time I gathered together a small mixed flock of goats, sheep and alpacas to keep the grass under control. I could move them from one side of the house to the other as they happily munched away. The alpacas proved to be worth their weight in gold; not only producing a magnificent fleece every year but also for being efficient fox-repellents, especially when lambs and kids were in the flock. Alpacas have a natural hatred for foxes and produce a blood-curdling cry if one enters the paddock, then they take after it at high speed.

Our animals were more decorative than practical. They kept the grass down, which in turn kept my hayfever under control. They ran to the fence to greet us whenever we were in the garden, and loved having the children around for extra pats and treats. The property also came with a flock of geese – I'd always been a bit nervous about these large birds because of their aggressive honking but ours were quite easy-going and friendly. They stayed around the house, nibbling the grass and occasionally laying eggs in small clutches. Not many of their progeny survived – foxes were the culprit.

Our son Ethan built an amazing straw bale chicken house – more of a palace than a shed – which was used primarily as a safe haven for them at night. He fenced off a huge run – half an acre at least – with a two-metre wall of chicken wire to keep the foxes out. We kept the newborn kids and lambs in this area with their mothers, again to keep them safe. Our chickens laid in the chicken house but also in hidden places within the huge run. It was great fun for the children to go on an egg hunt then have a delicious omelette for lunch.

There were lots of old fruit trees established around the farm, so I didn't really bother planting any more. Water was always an issue and I wanted to save it for the vegetable garden. Over time I had learned to grow our favourites – asparagus and redcurrants; always tomatoes and chillies in the summer; always broad beans and broccoli in winter. I loved growing potatoes – the Irish peasant in me – then digging them up and drying them in the shade. The children loved digging potatoes as well; it's an inherently dirty job and there's the magic of each turning of the fork to discover more creamy new spuds. I acknowledge that harvesting can be as time consuming as creating the garden itself. You need to factor in the time it will take to pick, pluck or dig up the produce and the messy aspect of cleaning it up before bringing it into the kitchen. The storage takes time as well. Potatoes gathered into sacks, stored in the dark. The tomatoes bottled or dried and stored in jars with garlic and oil. The garlic itself dried over many weeks then either plaited or stored in open-weave bags. The chillies made into a paste or also dried and stored in the dark. Freezing, bottling, jam-making, pickling – hours and hours of work but the flavour makes it all worthwhile. It's all about the taste of fresh, homegrown food. I can't live without it.

There's no point putting all that work into such a garden if you don't love cooking. It's one of my great joys and I see it as an act of love for the family. Every morning I lie in bed and think about what I will cook that day. Lunch and dinner. I ponder what's in the garden; what's in the pantry; what's in the fridge. I can't imagine why people find cooking a chore when it's such an adventure.

Mealtimes have always been happy times; the family together with good food and convivial conversation. The kind of life I always wanted. A big comfortable home in a beautiful setting that could accommodate all the family.

8

Preparing for the worst

THE FARM, MAY 2012

Our days leading up to David's first round of chemotherapy infusion are tranquil. I've stocked the pantry and freezer with delicacies and there's lots of fruit on the trees and vegetables in the garden. We sleep in, make love, walk around the farm and enjoy long lunches. I'm trying to fatten him up, of course, but he doesn't suspect my motives. I've taken it very personally, the specialist's prediction that David will die from starvation. I'm on a mission – at least I can ensure he's well-nourished during treatment. In my head I'm formulating an eating plan of meals so enticing, so luscious and nutritious, that he will gain weight during treatment rather than lose it.

If it's cold we have a snooze in the afternoon, cuddling up together with the fire crackling and the curtains drawn. We've never really allowed ourselves blissful time together like this and it's crazy that it took a drastic illness to force us to simply make time for ourselves.

My instinct is to create the most comfortable and comforting environment for David. Open fires lift our mood and force us out on morning walks to gather kindling and bring in logs from the woodshed. We also have to check on our animals – the goats, sheep, alpacas, geese, ducks and chickens – and David loves this. The irony is that he was really reluctant to leave our long-time home in Leura to come to the farm at Yetholme, yet now he loves the setting, the house and gardens and the animals. When he was first diagnosed with cancer, however, his initial reaction was to propose selling the farm and downsizing to a standard house on a quarter-acre block. I fervently disagreed, knowing that selling a home, buying another house and packing up and moving are among the most stressful of all undertakings (apart from death itself, and divorce.) I put my foot down.

'We need to rationalise our outgoings,' he insisted every time we went for a walk around the paddocks checking the fences. 'It costs a fortune to run this place and if neither of us is earning it's all money out and nothing coming in.'

'Packing up and selling this place while dealing with chemo will be a complete nightmare,' I countered. 'We love it here, we will stay here, we will not put ourselves through any additional angst.' I pleaded.

David takes refuge in his home office, emailing and talking to friends and work colleagues. In the beginning he was reluctant to let anyone 'in the industry' know that he was sick. He completely refused to tell anyone what was going on, even his closest working colleagues.

'You need to include people in this situation,' I kept saying. 'They will be tremendously loving and supportive. You have never needed their backing and understanding more than you do right now.'

He's been a great mentor and encourager of many young people working in film, and they would want to know he was sick, and want to help him stay positive and focused.

By nature a negative person, David is convinced that industry buzz and gossip will impact on the film and television projects he's working on, which are in various stages of development. This fear of failure worries him deeply. He believes he's letting down the side, threatening the projects of young writers, directors and actors he admires.

David sees his cancer as a flaw. A failing. He's always been such a strong and determined man, driven to succeed in one of the toughest of all industries. Now he feels all washed up; ready for the scrap heap. Despite my best efforts, I'm observing him slipping rapidly into melancholia. He blames himself, and his fury is cruelly self-directed. He has always carried around a lot of fear – a fear of failure in particular. Over our four decades together he has constantly worried about money, always very tough on himself when times were bad. It's difficult to deal with his state of mind; I find him sitting and staring into space. Sombre. I'm hoping it is part of his journey towards acceptance, and that soon he'll find some joy in his life.

Around this time a social worker from the cancer clinic decides to pay us a spontaneous visit. I admire social workers and the role they play, especially in this context of supporting people who are facing a long illness. Some people view them as interfering do-gooders, however I've always found them to be dedicated with a genuine desire to help people in the community. There is, of course, a fine line between offering help and sticking your nose in where it may not be wanted. It's all in the timing.

Regrettably, on the day she makes a journey out to the farm I'm over in the Blue Mountains speaking to a garden club – it's one of the residual commitments of my working life that I am loath to cancel. After a happy morning chatting to lovely gardeners and having cups of tea, sandwiches and friendly fellowship, I return to the farm to find David pacing the floor like a man deranged.

He launches into a furious tirade, and it takes me a while to understand what has transpired while I was absent.

The social worker arrived unannounced at the front door – which we rarely use – and it took him some time to hear her knocking from his office a long way down the corridor. Still in his pyjamas and dressing gown, he took her down to the kitchen for a cup of tea. She's the same woman who was sitting in on our depressing consultation with Dr Death, and she obviously picked up on our mood at the end of that particularly gruelling encounter.

After some small talk she launched into the real purpose of her visit, which was to discuss David's acceptance – or rather his lack of acceptance – of his inevitable demise. This was like waving a red rag at a bull.

I only have his side of the story, and that's harrowing enough. He described how he leaped to his feet, shouting (and probably banging on the kitchen table).

'I am NOT a stupid man,' he boomed. 'I fully understand the diagnosis and what is happening to me. But YOU have to understand that I am fighting this thing and I have no intention of just lying down and dying!'

At which point he launched loudly and theatrically into several verses of Dylan Thomas's 'Do not Go Gentle into That Good Night'.

By the time he got to 'Rage, rage against the dying of the light' I am certain the poor woman must have been feeling quite uncomfortable.

Things got worse.

'You HAVE to understand I intend fighting and I expect EVERYONE to fight with me. Those who are not fighting with me, are against me. They're my enemies. If you're one of those, then you're my enemy and I suggest you FUCK OFF RIGHT NOW.'

Which she did.

I try not to laugh as David passionately re-enacts this scene for my benefit, but of course I can't help myself. A large bear of a man with a bristling beard and deep, commanding voice – a remnant of the time he worked as an actor – he's always used his oratorical skills to great effect. Especially in moments of confrontation. I've heard many stories over the years of him jumping to his feet during business meetings when things were not going his way and delivering similar outrageous soliloquys.

That's the thing about David: he's larger than life and he's always, *always* grabbed every day by the horns. His sheer determination, probably fuelled by anger and a desire to succeed, has carried him through countless difficult situations. I can't help but admire his mental and physical strength and his tenacity. To my mind he's the last person who could possibly be felled by an illness such as this and I allow his unwavering self-belief to lull me into joining with him in a form of mutual self-delusion. It's exactly what the social worker was getting at, but at that moment it was a message we were quite obviously not at all ready to receive.

Afterwards, we take a long walk around the farm, enjoy yet another delicious lunch and fall into bed for an afternoon cuddle. I'm not looking forward to bumping into the social worker when we start the first chemotherapy at the clinic next Friday.

I can't help but wonder how the negative social worker encounter would have evolved if I had been at home on that day. Over many decades I've developed a way of dealing with David, who can be volatile and difficult, by diffusing his outbursts with humour. There were times when I resented having to do this dance of diffusion, to keep things on an even keel, because it harked back to my painful 'learned'

childhood behaviour patterns. As the youngest in a volatile and difficult family, very early I took on the role of peace-keeper and refined social strategies to prevent problems from escalating into huge dramas. Or physical fights.

I'm sure that the moment the social worker launched into her 'acceptance' mission speech I would've thrown David a 'look' that he'd recognise immediately: back off. Or if that failed, given his shin a sharp nudge with my foot under the table. Signals and body language that long-time married people recognise and (hopefully) respond to. Then I would've hijacked the conversation, made a few jokes and steered it in a different direction. It would not have ended in tears.

I've never felt even remotely intimidated by David during his vocal outbursts. In every way he's the opposite of my father – who terrified me when he lost control and who was relentless in his personal abuse. David's outbursts are never directed at me. Even if I'm deliberately provoking him or pushing the envelope, he will not retaliate in a personal or targeted way. He's always been melodramatic with overblown bluff and bluster. He can rave and rant and storm about the house, then five minutes later it's all over. I could never have stayed with him all these years if he had been abusive. Even if he was furious with me, I didn't once feel like the target of that fury.

It took me a long time to realise it, but David's intense and passionate nature is one of the things I love most about him. Everything in his world is either black or white and he always fiercely defends a particular viewpoint, even if it's irrational or bizarre. I've always tempered this approach with my more conciliatory nature. I hate confrontation and always want things to run smoothly. For everyone to be happy. In many ways my 'perfect' view of how life should be is delusional in itself, but it seems to have worked for more than forty years.

I recognise that David is not always a good listener; he's more inclined to react than to listen and think through a reasoned response. This character trait will follow him to the end.

9

Margaret

Between 2002 and 2012, I made frequent trips to Vancouver Island on the west coast of British Columbia. But not to take enthusiasts around gorgeous Canadian gardens. These trips were so I could spend precious time with my long lost older sister, Margaret.

My sister and I had a difficult story, both tragic and joyful, that went back to my very early childhood when Margaret was a teenager. She was my half-sister, nearly eighteen years my senior: we share a father, Theo. When she and her brother, Jon, were still under ten years old their mother, Veronica, died tragically of suicide. Within the family there has been much speculation about what led to this disaster, and I'm certain there were many causes including a depressive illness and the fact that she was quite far from her supportive family in Melbourne. Regardless, my journalist father's reckless behaviour – heavy drinking, irresponsible spending and womanising – were undoubtedly also a contributing factor.

Two or three years later our father met and married the woman who would later become my mother, Muriel Angel. She was a young trainee journalist and court reporter on the same daily paper where he was news editor. Although only twenty-one, she willingly took on those two unfortunate children and tried to make their lives as normal and happy as possible. It wasn't an easy task.

This all happened during the early stages of the Second World War, when my father was posted as a foreign correspondent to New York and Washington. Muriel and the children followed, and from all accounts it was a life-changing six years. Most certainly it must have been for the children. There are some beautiful black and white photographs of them taken in New York and rural Connecticut, where the family was based while Theo travelled across the country to Washington for his job.

I believe it was largely a happy time for them, however inevitably my father's behaviour patterns re-emerged and my mother, many years later, recounted some of the hair-raising incidents that occurred during that time in the States. There were humdinger fights and domestic violence – massive drinking binges and socialising with the upmarket Connecticut social set. An exciting, outrageous but ultimately damaging period in their lives.

Back in Australia after the war, my brother Dan was born, followed in rapid succession by me and a baby sister,

Jane. All within three years. My parents had a tense and at times hostile relationship and it was a fraught time for all of us. Our mother had also become a heavy drinker after the years living the high life in America, and she continued drinking and smoking right through these three pregnancies, births and afterwards. She wasn't a bad person – far from it – and I always felt greatly loved by her despite the dysfunctional nature of our family. Back then, doctors didn't advise pregnant women about the dangers of alcohol and smoking – the facts weren't understood. Baby Jane died in hospital before her first birthday and although I have a copy of her death certificate, I really don't know exactly why she died.

My half-brother, Jon, became a marine engineer and went to sea, and Margaret was training to be an art teacher when she dramatically did a runner from the family home. She had no further contact with us, although both Jon and my mother tried to track her down at various times. Through distant family connections we eventually discovered she'd achieved her goal to become an art teacher and that she'd moved to Canada, but that was all we knew.

Growing up, I always wondered about my sister, perhaps because Mum spoke of her with such affection. I knew she was a talented artist with a sweet, gentle disposition. When I first hooked up to the internet I tried searching for her through various universities and institutions across the country, without success. I only had her maiden name – Margaret Mary Moody – and Canada is a mighty big place. I had no success at all.

When at the age of fifty I took off for France and wrote a memoir about my experiences titled *Au Revoir*, I talked quite a lot about my sister and my quest to reconnect with her. I wrote:

> Margaret's sudden disappearance from our lives had a profound impact on me. I feel certain she must have been the primary carer for me during that period when our sister Jane was dying. I often lay in bed at night, listening to my parents brawling in the living room, and fantasising that my sister Margaret would walk back through the door and rescue me. It never happened. I dreamt of her vividly for decades.

After the book was published, I did an interview with journalist Geraldine Doogue on her radio program *Life Matters*. She was particularly interested in our complex family story, including my search for my long-lost sister. I explained how I had tried finding her in earnest but that I had no idea whether she'd married and was no longer using her maiden name.

Later that day, I had a call from Geraldine's radio production office to say they had been contacted by a woman in Western Australia who claimed to be a friend of Margaret's. She told the researchers that she had an address for her and was willing to pass it on. The physical effect of this phone call was dramatic. I was standing in front of my desk and my knees literally went from under me. I was suddenly on the floor trying to gather myself to write down the woman's contact details. It took me a while to be calm enough to make that critical call; I was determined not to cry. Margaret's friend was delightful and told me a little bit about her life on Vancouver Island and of her marriage. It was difficult to speak coherently but I did my best.

Now I had an address, I finally knew how to find her, and I wrote a long, long letter to my sister. I enclosed a copy of *Au Revoir*, because she was so much a part of my story, my childhood and my sense of loss.

Within a week I had a letter back from my Margaret. When I reached for it in our old rural mailbox, and realised it was from her, yet again I went weak at the knees. Sitting on the grassy verge outside the farm gate I read it once, and then again. In the back of my mind I had been worrying she would not reply. That too much time had passed and that she might want to keep her family at arm's length.

Not so! Her letter was filled with surprise and delight. She was excited to have heard from me; she was so pleased that I was happy and enjoying my life; she was hoping we could reunite. She said that she had started to read the book but couldn't continue; the memories it stirred were too painful. She would try again after Christmas, and then write back to me with her feelings about what I had written. I had to suppress an overwhelming urge to just get on the next plane to Vancouver and arrive unannounced at her front doorstep. I sent her and her husband Ken a Christmas card, and asked for their phone number. My entire family were excited for me, especially David. He knew so well my sadness over many decades at having 'lost' my sister. He had the seen the old black and white photographs I had of Margaret, which I treasured. Finding her was something I'd wanted so much for such a long time, and now it was happening.

Christmas and New Year came and went and I heard nothing more from my sister. January and then February and I was becoming concerned but didn't want to pester her by writing again. Had she changed her mind? Had she read the book and decided against any further contact? In March a second letter arrived – a long and detailed letter full of love and lots of information. She opened with an apology: 'I had many things to do with Christmas coming so I put your book and letter away in a safe place. Guess what? I forgot where that was. I finally found it two days ago. I'd put it with some art supplies in a very conspicuous place. Humph! I'm afraid I have blindness of the mind.'

How poignant are those words knowing now what was to emerge. In this first long letter in which she described in great detail, page after page, the events of the decades since we had separated, she is hinting at her forgetfulness. Her 'blindness of the mind'.

Her letter gave me many clues to her true character. Describing her first teaching job at an Australian inner-city high school, she wrote: 'The kids were rough and tough but a great start for any novice teacher'. Later, she described her first teaching job at a university in Canada, where 'The students were very polite, obedient and boring. Maybe the cold weather shapes their personalities'. This made me laugh out loud. Further on she described moving to Vancouver Island where

'I was an assistant professor in art education and I was delighted to find my students were cheeky and challenging'.

I sensed Margaret was a placid person. Even when writing about the deep pain of our shared childhoods, it was without overt emotion. She had a certain matter-of-factness about her style. In that sense she was very different from me.

Several months later when I met my sister face to face for the first time in forty-eight years, I was to discover we had more in common than I could have ever imagined. I caught a plane from Australia to Los Angeles, connecting to a flight to Vancouver. The flight from LA was delayed and I nearly missed the small plane that would take me on the twenty-minute hop to Vancouver Island. I ran like a madwoman to catch this plane, my heart in my mouth. After nearly five decades I was frantic in my need to be with her, on time. I was also determined not to cry when I saw Margaret. I had to be more like her. Exhausted from the long journey, but pumped with adrenaline, I emerged from the landing gate and saw them standing together – Margaret and her husband, Ken. He was very tall and she was much smaller than me, a bird of a woman with a halo of white hair and a broad smile.

'Gidday,' she said, and we hugged. I did cry, like a fool.

Back at her farmhouse we talked and talked. She had so many stories to tell me from her childhood (before I was born) and the time they spent in New York. She told me how my mother cared for them so tenderly despite being not much more than a girl herself when she married Dad. The lives of Margaret and Jon had been shattered when their mother died. Margaret was only seven at the time. Muriel was always an affectionate woman and helped a lot in their healing. But they never fully recovered from the trauma.

Every evening we would sit talking after dinner and she would share a new chapter of her story, helping me to understand her reasons for abandoning our family and having no further contact with us.

'I was fed up with the constant fights,' she said and I nodded with understanding.

Like me, she was frightened whenever there was a fight, especially when it became violent. She told me that during their time in America she had often intervened when our father was physically attacking Muriel. She must have been a very brave young woman to have tried to come between them. She also told me, with some amusement, the story of our father writing to the headmistress of her high school, suggesting that Margaret should leave school because she was needed at home to care for her younger siblings (my brother and me). It was at a time when Dad was having an affair and my mother was drinking heavily. Margaret was a brilliant student and the principal's reaction was one of outrage. She phoned our father at his work and blasted him about 'destroying his daughter's future'. Like most bullies he backed off very quickly, but it made Margaret feel even more uncomfortable at home.

She said she felt guilty leaving my brother and me behind in what she believed was an untenable situation. Yet she needed to save herself. Dad never forgave her and by the time he died she was living on the other side of the world.

'After that I felt I had just left it too long to re-establish any contact,' she said. 'I suppose I was worried about what I might find if came back.'

I completely understood her dilemma.

Margaret laughed like me, our smiles were so alike and our voices sounded so similar that when David phoned the morning after I arrived and Margaret answered, he thought it was me. How could she have lived in Canada for more than thirty years and still sound like an Aussie? Her sense of humour as well − she was quick-witted with a wickedly wry take on life. We fell in together naturally, picking up the threads of our disparate lives. She loved farming life (ditto), making compost, arranging flowers, making jam and wearing a straw hat . . . ditto, ditto, ditto. How is it that two of the tablecloths in her linen cupboard were the same as ones I had at home? The same sort of old-fashioned furniture. She was generous and kind and funny. I wish we'd known each other all our lives, not just at the beginning and the end.

I liked her husband Ken. Softly spoken and gentle, he seemed astonished that another version of his wife had appeared out of the blue. He listened while we talked and laughed and shared our myriad stories. He invited his extended family around to meet me and I helped Margaret cook up a huge, delicious feast. We sat side by side at the dinner table, doing a sister's double act. It brought the house down!

But I was surprised at how hesitant she was in her daily routines. As a woman who'd had such a high-powered career she seemed lacking in confidence even at the smallest of tasks. That evening we cooked dinner for Ken's family was a case in point. She planned a simple meal of soup, a roast dinner and dessert. The soup and the pudding were made in advance, so we really only had to prepare and cook the main course. I set the table and joined her in the kitchen to peel the vegetables. We talked and laughed as we worked together but at times Margaret seemed rather overwhelmed and she was hopeless at pointing me to various utensils in the kitchen.

'Where's the potato peeler live?' I asked and she started rifling through drawers trying to find it. The same with the colander and the masher. Yet later in the evening when we were tidying up and putting away the clean dishes and cutlery she seemed to know the correct place for everything. In truth the kitchen and pantry were very orderly, so her inability to quickly lay her hands on a particular object when needed appeared contradictory.

Imagine how devastated I was then, when less than two years after re-establishing this wonderful connection with Margaret, she was diagnosed with early onset Alzheimer's. She was the same age then as I am now, as I write this. Sixty-eight. I felt angry about all those years we'd missed; and terrified of how the illness would progress. With David's full support I scaled back my work and travel to become her part-time carer, and over a period of six years I spent nearly three years living and helping out at their farm. I felt it was the least I could do; that she deserved to be well loved through this terrible disease. The first part of her life had been so traumatic and damaging, I was determined that the end of her life was going to be as good as I could possibly make it.

10

David

David's been going to the Cannes Film Festival on the Côte d'Azur in France with the Australian contingent since the late 1970s when his earliest films were produced and released. He usually heads to France the second week of May, but this year he must cancel this annual pilgrimage because that's the week he will begin his first round of chemotherapy.

His annual attendance at the flashy festival reflects his obsessive love of routine and ritual. Once he stumbles across something that pleases him, he's inclined to repeat that joyful experience time and time again. He's become an institution at the Cannes Film Festival.

It's an opportunity to network, to tout for funding for future film projects on his slate, and to mix creatively with new young writers and directors in the hope of ultimately working with them. This approach has certainly been effective: several of his most interesting and applauded films were a direct result of contacts and associations made during the frantic twelve days that is Cannes.

While it sounds glamorous and expensive, David worked hard to make it a success and he knew how to do it all on a shoestring budget. He prided himself on spending as little money as possible (not just at Cannes – in every aspect of his life) and he'd evolved a strategy over the decades where he shared very basic digs in the back streets with a small group of not-quite-famous-yet international identities. Known as the 'boys' dorm', eight or more people would be packed into a suite normally designed for three or four.

David hasn't missed a festival in thirty-three years, but as we sit by the fire after dinner on the eve of his first chemotherapy assault, he hints sadly to me that he may never return to that beloved stomping ground. The festival is due to start in just ten days.

'I'm trying not to think about France,' he says. 'It all just seems impossible now.'

This breaking of a time-honoured routine is the first chink in his armour. It's the first time he's acknowledged that his life is about to change. It frightens me to hear him utter the words, and I make light of them.

'Surely you will be fine by this time next year. The chemo will have long finished and you will be feeling strong again.'

Was I in denial or just trying to cheer him up?

I hate the thought that something that has brought him so much pleasure and kudos could be all over.

David's fastidious management of money didn't arise from stinginess, but from a parsimonious Scottish upbringing on his mother's side. Although they were a conservative and well-off family, there was an abiding dislike of financial ostentation or wastefulness. David's handsome actor father, who was more relaxed about spending money, was considered 'flashy' by his wife's side of the family – a view that was maintained through his parents' entire married life.

This ability to make money last with careful economy has always stood him in good stead within the local film industry. David was capable of administrating huge production budgets – often in the multimillions – and ensuring that every film he produced came in on time and well within budget. Quite a feat when you consider the endless possibilities for disaster during the film making process – accidents on set, actors falling ill or having a meltdown, disputes between departments vying for a larger slice of the pie. Unforeseen weather.

Yet David was much more than just a numbers man, a glorified accountant. He loved all aspects of the creative process from collaborating with the screenwriter to working on casting and locations with the director and the finer details of music and art direction. He was great at delegating responsibility but also quite capable of stepping in firmly if any area of the production was falling behind. He never missed rushes in the evening, was on the film set or location several times a day (often to coincide with meals being served by the catering trucks) and was totally involved in the post-production – the editing and sound mixing were as important to him as the script and the casting.

This absolute immersion in his craft meant he was away from me and his family for lengthy periods of time – weeks and endless months when he'd be completely absorbed in the task at hand. I greatly respected this dedication and the fact that he took so much pride and pleasure in his career. Even though at times I found it a struggle to keep life at home on an even keel – a large family, a big house and garden and a demanding fulltime job – I'd rather have had a passionate husband than one who was vaguely bored or frustrated in a routine nine-to-five job.

In contrast, my attitude to money was formed by an entirely opposing set of childhood circumstances. My father and mother both worked and both earned high salaries, yet we lived fortnight to fortnight. They never bought a house – we lived in the same rented flat until I was sixteen when they contributed a small amount to a house being bought in the same suburb by my recently divorced brother Jon. Except for a brief period when my father inherited money following the death of his mother in Melbourne, we were permanently short of cash. Bills were not opened but stuffed away out of sight in a drawer. Debt collectors sometimes came knocking on a Sunday morning. I can't really say where all the money went – our only family holidays were staying with family friends who owned farms and we didn't own a car or television until I was nearly ten years old. Money was just frittered away. My father indulged in smart handmade Italian wool suits and expensive shirts and ties; he gambled on the Saturday horse races and was a member of an exclusive inner-city gymnasium. Both our parents were excellent cooks and they always used the most expensive ingredients so our household food bills were always high. A large percentage of the income went on alcohol and cigarettes.

I inherited this casual approach to expenditure and it's caused plenty of friction in my relationship with David over the decades. I've never spent much money on myself – my clothes, shoes or hairstyles – it was more about making our home comfortable and welcoming. Largesse in food and wine; a generosity of spirit. Our garden always sucked up a lot of money, as did books, newspapers and journals. While David loved being part of this lifestyle, it also made him very nervous. The film industry is precarious at the best of times – good money can be made when a film has been financed and is in production. But there were always lengthy droughts between films – sometimes years and years with no income. Just outgoings.

So my earnings as a jobbing journalist, author and trek leader were fundamental to our survival. We could rely on a steady income from my freelance work, and that held the fort between film projects. But David's constant concern about our future, about surviving financially in such a competitive and at times ruthless climate, has caused no end of stress.

The cancer treatment clinic in Bathurst is sunny and welcoming. The oncology nurses there are marvellous women; gentle and kind, humorous and helpful. David is taken into a warm room with big windows facing west, shaded by a handsome old tree. He's made comfortable in a well-padded reclining chair and a port is inserted into a vein in his left arm. I note that the nurses are wearing protective clothing over their uniforms – a sort of plastic shield – to prevent the risk of being splashed or splattered by any of the chemicals in the mix called Taxol that will be pumped into David's body.

There are cheerful volunteers bringing us cups of tea and sandwiches – it's a very homey, convivial atmosphere. I leave him to get on with it for an hour while I go shopping. Living twenty-five minutes from town means we don't 'pop to the shops' every day, so this is a good opportunity to stock up the pantry for the weeks ahead. Back at the clinic we eat the homemade soup and bread that I brought with us and chat with the nurses until the dose has been fully delivered. There is nothing traumatic about the process.

We go home and I watch him closely for adverse reactions or side effects. Nothing. He just gets on with his normal evening routine. I google Taxol and am bemused to learn it's a drug derived from one of my favourite conifers, the yew tree.

The species *Taxus brevifolia*, Pacific yew, is a native under-storey tree of the western forests of the United States. I'm more familiar with the European yews and know yews are toxic, but have no idea about their medicinal uses. However I'm not really surprised to discover that long ago the bark was boiled to produce an elixir to induce miscarriage. It had been an abortion drug. Modern chemistry has developed a compound obtained from the bark which is extremely effective in treating solid tumour cancers. One of the websites looks at the symbolism of the yew. As well as being an obvious symbol of death, they also represent the cycle of life and are a symbol of rebirth because a new tree grows from the decaying trunk of the old one.

It seems curious to me that a much-admired tree which I've photographed on my overseas garden tours is now part of David's cancer regime. I study the sheet we were given at the clinic that lists the possible side effects of Taxol. It's a long list, but we'll jump these problems if and when they occur. David hasn't shown any interest in reading all this extra information in the factsheets and booklets that we are constantly given. He hasn't googled anything; he hasn't asked any questions or sought out any alternatives to conventional mainstream treatments. He appears to have entirely handed himself over to the medical profession and is placing all his trust in whatever is recommended. This seems such a contradiction to me, given his usually inquiring mind and pleasure at thumbing his nose at convention. It must be a form of self-protection: the less he reads or knows, the less he will worry.

He's well aware that I'm doggedly reading everything I can find on the subject; spending hours on the internet, making lists of questions and posing alternative ideas. This is now my role, to be his advocate and advisor.

He, on the other hand, has decided the best therapy will be complete distraction. He loves film, and our local cinema has five screens. So instead of swimming lengths of the pool every day, as he has done for many years, his plan is to see absolutely every new film that's released. Over the next twelve months we do just that. Hours and hours spent in the dark, eating choc-tops and escaping the reality that is our new life.

During this lengthy chemotherapy we struggle to communicate about the reality of the situation. My problem isn't the physical side of David's illness. He seems to be coping valiantly, still getting up early every day to make coffee for himself and a pot of tea for me. When you live with a person of rituals, it can be both amusing and wearing. Every action follows a precise order: trip to the bathroom followed by walk to the office to switch on the computer: kettle on and coffee machine filled with water and grounds. The pot is heated, the bread sliced and into the toaster. Two scoops of tea leaves, boiling water. Butter the toast, pour in milk then the tea, through a strainer. He brings me the tea and toast, smiles and then stays to watch me take the first sip.

'How is it?' he asks, every single day.

As this tea ceremony has been perfected, he should know it's exactly as I like it. But he still needs to ask. I usually just smile and say, 'Perfect, thanks darling'.

But some days I can't resist wrinkling my nose just to shake him up a bit. It amazes me that even after all these decades, he still can't recognise when I'm teasing him. When I laugh, he laughs. Funny old bloke.

The worry I have with David is his overall reaction to his illness. Gradually he's started to share the news with his closest colleagues and has been inviting them to come to the farm and visit – to spend time and hang out. I'm delighted with this idea, knowing the love and support they will offer. Yet he's filled with despair at the thought that he's letting these people down, that he's failing them in terms of getting their projects into production. He becomes obsessed with this notion, and most of his days (apart from when we drive to town to see a movie) are spent lamenting the hand he has been dealt, and the impact it's having on the people he works with.

I can't help but be irked by this lack of balance. Not once has he mentioned the impact his illness and probable death is having on me, on our four children and ten grandchildren, his siblings and other family members. It's all about his work and his perceived failings.

Long ago I accepted that David's a workaholic, driven to prove himself and to succeed. We've talked about it so often – usually in bed on a Sunday morning, always our most serene time together. He puts it down to his troubled relationship with his father, who returned injured during the war and was thereafter a difficult, demanding man. Despite having been an actor himself, his father was scathing about David's career direction – first as an actor and then as a producer of television and film. I remember visiting his family in New Zealand and his father referring to David – then well into his thirties – as the 'boy wonder'. I sensed it was a put down. So did David.

The disapproval of a parent is damaging. David has always been very tough on himself. He takes life pretty seriously and often questions my philosophy that life is meant to be fun. He doesn't get it – he seems to quite enjoy doing without fun. Not quite sackcloth and ashes, but almost.

I attempt to have discussions about setting priorities, about looking at and appreciating all the fantastic things he accomplished in his life; and the love that is surrounding him. Our wonderful home, our terrific family, our combined career highs. He's won dozens of industry awards and accolades but even seeing these trophies sitting on a mantelpiece is no comfort to him.

I just cannot seem to break through. I can cope with him being angry and railing against the injustice of the disease. I can't cope when he's hangdog, self-pitying and indulgently negative.

We both have our own offices at the farm – his is the smallest bedroom that we converted into a cosy workroom and mine the glassed-in veranda with lovely views through the arboretum to the creek. David frequently stays too long in his office – the dinner will be cooked and I'll be waiting for him to come out and join me for a drink and a few minutes of watching the news before we eat. I have often sent him an email:

> Remember me? I'm that red-headed woman who lives here and I'm gagging for a gin and tonic.

He'd immediately close down his computer and scurry out, mix us a drink and we'd sit cuddled up in front of the television.

However, after weeks of dealing with his gloomy and joyless demeanour, I sent him a missive in a completely different tone:

> I'm writing to you in the hope that some of the things I say will have some effect. Talking doesn't seem to be working.
>
> It was 5 April when Dr Death announced that you had, on average, twelve months to live.
>
> I don't believe this – any more than you do (or should).
>
> But many weeks have passed. The radiotherapy treatment and the time at Lilier Lodge were hugely beneficial. However, you have made no progress in terms of trying to rationalise the situation, to harden-the-fuck-up and move forward.
>
> If Dr Death is right then you have just wasted one-twelfth of your time left on this earth. I will keep writing these emails until you agree to start enjoying your life.

You've spent the last seventy-two years giving yourself hell. Can't you stop now PLEASE and try to have some happy times for all of us to enjoy?

Your not-very-long-suffering wife.

I didn't need to send another email. Looking back, I'm appalled that I sent such a strongly worded letter, given the grim situation he was facing. But I needed to shake him up. To change his perspective.

After all this time, searching my old email files I can find no response to my outburst. I honestly can't recall us ever talking about it afterwards. I just know that his attitude does change from that day onwards. He opens up, starts to look around and see the world again. It's a huge relief. The last thing I want is to be fighting him at a time when I know he needs my unequivocal love and support. It's just too important for me to allow this bleak and self-punishing state of mind to continue.

11

Vancouver Island

Looking back at it all, I realise that my relationship with David could not be more different from my sister Margaret's relationship with her husband, Ken.

As a 'runaway' who'd abandoned her painful Australian life and found refuge and happiness on beautiful Vancouver Island, Margaret had remained single into her mid-thirties. Then she met Ken, who was eight years older. Both teachers who loved classical music, they met at a symphony concert. Ken was painfully shy, a bachelor who was very keen to meet the right woman, settle down and have a family.

Margaret was lonely too, and finally ready for the sort of love and support that such a marriage could bring. Some years earlier, however, she'd decided not to have children, undoubtedly because of her own traumatic childhood experiences; her sense of loss and abandonment after the sudden death of her mother and my father's self-destructive, alcoholic view of the world. So in her late twenties she had a tubal ligation to prevent the possibility of an unwanted pregnancy. It's uncommon for doctors to perform sterilisation surgery on young women but I'm certain Margaret would have been very persuasive: intelligent, charming and insistent. She never regretted the decision and she told me about it when we were first reunited.

However, when she told Ken that children would not be a factor in their relationship, he was deeply upset. He loved Margaret – that was without question – but he also wanted to be father. The relationship just drifted – he wouldn't commit to marriage under those circumstances. They were living together and I'm sure Margaret wasn't too fussed about formal marriage, but when Ken won a place in an over-forties rugby tour to the UK, he wanted Margaret to travel with him. They'd had a low-key marriage ceremony and jetted off to Europe. Ken was quite conservative and didn't feel he could take Margaret travelling unless she was his wife.

Instead of having a family Margaret threw herself into academia, gaining two masters degrees and then a doctorate of education. She became an associate professor at the University of Victoria and was very involved in the local art scene. Ken continued to play rugby and was also intensely interested in agriculture. Together they bought a small farm, planning to establish a kiwifruit plantation.

In her fifties Margaret was diagnosed with breast cancer, underwent a double mastectomy and decided to take early retirement from the university. Ken also retired and they built a lovely, spacious farmhouse on their land and planted several acres of fruit. It was an idyllic lifestyle – Ken joined the local agricultural society, they were growing most of their own vegetables and were very involved in the famous annual Saanich Fair. Margaret was a member of a serious weekly art group which held regular exhibitions. She made jams to enter in competition at the fair and she was very active in organisations that financially supported Indigenous education. It was during this period that I reconnected with Margaret.

In spite of her successful career and lively social network, Margaret was emotionally fragile. I only really understood this as I got to know her better, and as I became her part-time carer after her Alzheimer's diagnosis. It changed everything in her life, and most fundamentally her relationship with her husband.

Margaret had been loving and welcoming to Ken's extended family. Having severed her own family connections, she embraced his ageing parents, his cousins and nephews and their families. Ken couldn't speak highly enough of Margaret's devotion to the care of his mother and father towards the end of their lives, making meals, running errands and always being available when they needed assistance. She and Ken had regular family parties – lunches, dinners, barbecues, Christmas and New Year's parties for the family. They hosted family weddings in their garden and contributed financially to help family members when needed. This brought Margaret great joy.

When I suddenly arrived on the scene as the 'long-lost

sister' the family could not have been more astonished and delighted. Margaret hadn't mentioned her family or talked about any aspect of her previous life in Australia. They were wonderfully welcoming to me as they could see how thrilled Margaret was to have reconnected with her little sister.

Ken was incredibly protective of his wife and after her diagnosis he was determined at all costs to keep her living at home. In the beginning he coped pretty well, although every time I visited – usually twice a year – I could see that the situation was slowly deteriorating. Margaret's behaviours were baffling and frustrating. While we could still have a lively conversation with her, she was increasingly repeating herself and getting confused and anxious about everyday things. I detected that Ken was becoming frustrated and irritable with her, especially if she hid things. Car keys were her favourite. If keys were left on the kitchen bench they'd vanish – sometimes never to be seen again. Ken would explode, screaming at Margaret, which of course wasn't helpful as she didn't understand. I tried to work out strategies – hiding the keys somewhere out of reach – but these explosions of temper were becoming more regular and concerning.

The fine balance in any relationship can be altered if one partner becomes sick, and this was certainly happening here. Margaret had been a powerful personality, making many of the day-to-day household decisions, organising holidays and taking charge of most social situations. Ken's forte was running the farm and so, like most couples, they had developed their own roles and responsibilities.

Once Ken was thrown into the position of decision maker, he took it very seriously. Even though I could see he only wanted the best for Margaret, the shift of power changed the atmosphere in the house. He became controlling, making sure everything was done exactly as he wanted; he was critical of the part-time carers and local doctors. Eventually he started to be critical of friends and family members. Dealing with his behaviour became more difficult than dealing with Margaret herself.

During this stage Ken started talking to me a lot more, confiding in me about his marriage and his family relationships. Usually I would stay for six or eight weeks at a time, and he had become quite controlling about me and my movements. He didn't like me going out alone or meeting up with other people, and he was very anxious about household expenditure, insisting we all go shopping together and putting things I had chosen back on the shelves if he thought them extravagant. I took to sneaking out early and shopping separately; the irony was that he thoroughly enjoyed the meals I made, which were very different from the frugal recipes he prepared when I was not around.

What I didn't know – what no one knew – was that Ken was in the early stages of Parkinson's disease. It was only diagnosed eighteen months before Margaret's death, and even then he didn't accept the diagnosis or the prognosis (a bit like David). I was unknowingly dealing with a man in the grips of a neurological condition with many variables and contradictions; a condition that can take numerous twists and turns and which has a profound effect on personality.

As Margaret's condition deteriorated, and her language skills decreased, Ken became more and more domineering. Suddenly he enjoyed criticising Margaret, not in her current condition, but casting his mind back over the years of their marriage. He talked about Margaret's repeated mental breakdowns. I'd never heard anything about these episodes, however years later, in their shared bathroom cabinet, I stumbled across dozens of half-empty bottles of prescription medications such as Valium and similar anti-anxiety drugs. Ken was a hoarder and had never thrown away any of these meds with 'use by' dates going back decades. Looking at these dates I could detect a pattern. Every two or three years Margaret would be given a script, she would take about a third of the drugs and then obviously abandon them. I knew her to be a health fanatic, not wanting to even take Panadol for a headache. She would have hated being fuzzed out by this medication.

One afternoon Ken said, 'I really like Margaret much better now than when she could talk. She's much easier to live with.'

I was horrified and utterly confused. What was he saying? That he preferred my beautiful sister to be mute, robbed of her mental powers? Was he saying he was happier now because he was the one in control?

It changed the way I felt about everything and made me worried for my sister's ongoing welfare in ways I couldn't describe. I had always looked forward to my visits with excitement and joy; now a grey cloud hung over the pretty farmhouse on Vancouver Island.

12

Therapy times

As predicted, David is hit hard by the second round of chemotherapy in early June. His skin's colour and texture change, turning grey and waxy. His hair and beard begin falling out in clumps on the pillow and in the shower. Descended from the Scottish Picts, tribal Celtic warriors, he has always been pleased with his hairiness. His beard in particular has always been luxuriant and over the decades it has turned grey and then eventually silver. He keeps his hair and beard neatly trimmed and fastidiously tended. He is, like many men, quite vain about his appearance.

Chemotherapy drugs attack and destroy rapidly dividing cells, targeting the tumours but also affecting hair follicles, which are also very active structures that divide to produce the hair growth. David doesn't just lose his beard and the hair on his head – his eyebrows, eyelashes and body hair is shed over several weeks. He doesn't want to interfere in this process or to tidy himself up. It's as though the dramatic change in external appearance is a metaphor for what's happening inside his body. We just observe it and don't really discuss it. I pick up the clumps of hair in the shower and change the bedding every couple of days.

He also feels lethargic and apathetic, however the nausea drugs are effective enough for him to continue eating. His appetite's robust but his tastebuds have changed, leaving a metallic sensation in the mouth. I counter this by making our meals richer and tastier, often very spicy. The intense flavours and heat of the chilli somehow counterbalance the metallic taste. Our food is deliberately high in fats and carbohydrates, with lots of vegetables from the garden to help maintain his weight.

During these chemo months there's a lot of comfort eating and drinking. Never much of a drinker, David is now having an aperitif gin and tonic before lunch and again before our evening meal. I guzzle wine at lunchtime and again at night. We often sleep in the afternoon then go for a walk if the weather is pleasant. It's so convivial; the rhythm of the days is gentle and we feel no pressure or anxiety. We are lulled into a sense that everything will just continue like this: the two of us at the farm, enjoying each other's company, sometimes going to town to see a film and always looking forward to weekend visits from friends and family.

Looking back, it's curious that during this time death was never discussed. We know it's there as a constant, but we push it to the periphery of our daily routine. When someone is alive and sitting beside you on the sofa and you are talking, you don't really want to initiate a conversation about what life will look like when they are no longer around. We do a lot of reminiscing, about the lovely times when the children were young, but also the bad times that are inevitable in any long-term relationship. In particular we talk a lot about the chapter, more than ten years before, when I lost the plot and fell in love with another man in France, and wrote about it with David's blessing in *Last Tango in Toulouse*.

David seems to take comfort in going over this major event in our lives. Pulling it all apart, putting it all back together. For me, the memories of this experience are mostly traumatic, so reliving them in conversation is sometimes painful. David seems to need to clarify it again and again, while I'd prefer to lay it all to rest. It denotes the differences between us – I'm more head-in-the-sand; he's more of a confronter.

It's also puzzling that in spite of my frequent outrageous behaviour during that time, David did not lay any blame at my feet. In his eyes, none of this was my fault or even my responsibility. Instead he blamed himself for emotional neglect and physical absence in the years leading up to the affair; he blamed the other man for taking advantage of my vulnerability; he blamed menopause, midlife crisis, empty nest syndrome. Just not me. He has always enjoyed the naughty side of my nature and he saw this as just another example of my tendency to be a bit badly behaved. A bit wild.

A psychologist would probably have a field day analysing this relationship twist. Was it because the 'good' part of me far outweighed my 'bad' or negative attributes? Did he vicariously enjoy my need for adventure? Certainly, he'd taken delight and nurtured my desire to do things that were edgy, maybe even risky. I'd always been full of big ideas and bold enthusiasms and he'd unquestioningly supported them. He never thwarted my need for a 'larger than life' life. If I wanted to give birth in the front room instead of going to hospital . . . go for it! If I wanted to take treks into the Himalayas, completely out of communication range . . . fantastic! If I wanted to live alone for six months in a remote French village . . . do it! Make a documentary about a French restaurant . . . why not? He was the one who made all these things possible. He was my enabler.

I knew I was adventurous and energetic, full of drive with high expectations of myself. I suspect that's what David found attractive and was willing to support. He was also, quite obviously, prepared to accept the downside and the consequences of his wife's fearless lifestyle. It wasn't until well after his death that I truly recognised and was deeply grateful for the gift of tolerance he'd given me.

13

love and madness

2002

My affair with the man in France was a form of insanity. When I look back on it, I still think of him as the third love of my life. He came from a different world and a culture that I obviously didn't understand. He was exotic and therefore intriguing to me. He was fun-loving and extravagant and also a risk-taker. We were both married and the forbidden aspect of our liaison heightened its intensity. Although I was besotted, I can't say that I loved everything about this man. His politics were repugnant to me, so I steered clear of conversations in this area. I was reluctant to argue with him so I just avoided the issue. I once laughingly confessed to him that it felt as though I was 'sleeping with the enemy' – undoubtedly this taboo compounded the attraction for both of us. I was infatuated, not just with him but with the whole notion of our clandestine assignations. I frequently asked myself '*What the hell are you doing?*' I knew I was not the first and undoubtedly wouldn't be the last of his extramarital affairs, yet at the height of our ardour this didn't bother me at all.

In every sense I was deliberately stepping away from my sense of self and from all that I held most dear. My family, my husband, my love of my home in Australia and my personal ethics. Was I running away from myself and everything I valued? Or was I just revelling in being a bad girl? Probably both.

I had a curious self-justification. I had never done anything like this before and I was loving the thrill of it. I kept telling myself '*It's now or never*'. I was egging myself on.

The long separations between my trips to France also contributed to the urgency of the affair. We were in constant long-term communication, planning our trysts and keeping the fervour alive. It was a game, a dangerous and addictive game that I was reluctant to abandon. The fact that once David discovered my betrayal he did not react with immediate outrage but with sadness and understanding, allowed me to continue. It took years before my lover and I came to our senses and it was only when David threw up his hands in despair and packed his bags that I knew I had to make a final decision and end the relationship once and for all.

After it was all over I gazed back at the entire episode with ambivalence. I certainly regretted the pain it caused to David in particular and I still have a muddled understanding of what was really going on in my head at the time. I couldn't see it then, but the personality similarities between my lover and my late father are undeniable. Both men charming, intelligent, persuasive, witty and manipulative. Both men serial womanisers and drunks. My relationship with my father ended very badly. I had adored him as a child even though I was frightened of his unpredictable temper and irrational outbursts. When he caused so much heartbreak to my mother I grew to loathe him to the point that I felt little but relief when he killed himself aged 62. This unresolved and painful relationship could perhaps have a bearing on the attraction I felt and my compulsion to pursue the relationship. Once again, a psychologist could have a field day.

14

A French fantasy

When I ran away from home at the age of fifty, to live in a small French village, I was looking for escape and relaxation – in truth real estate was the last thing on my mind. While I was there for six months I explored the region, soaked up the history and culture and made dozens of new friends, both French and expats. I also wrote a book, *Au Revoir: Running away from home at fifty*, which explained my need to make such a dramatic escape from my 'real life' at such a crucial age. I really thrived in this environment and enjoyed freedoms that I never could have imagined during those decades as working mother with a demanding career. The euphoria of waking up in the morning and thinking 'What will I do today?' The fun of meeting up with new friends and spending hours over a lingering lunch in a French workers' café. The simple joy of going on a country drive and discovering ancient fortified villages and ruined chateaux. The local food markets; the antique fairs, the village feast days. I couldn't abide the thought of never experiencing this way of life again and I knew that, if I just packed up and left France, my 'real' life would overtake me and engulf my time once again. Without a house of my own in France I would find it very difficult to get back and recapture the joys I had experienced.

I made an international call to David, reverse charges from a public phone booth, and proposed the idea of buying 'a very cheap cottage'. He was astonished at how modestly priced the houses were and I started looking around and phoning him with my discoveries – I had a laptop computer but neither of us were on the internet or using email back then. Eventually he decided to just come and see for himself, spend two weeks in France looking at houses with me and then we would then both fly back to Australia to be reunited with the family for Christmas.

David's reaction to the places I had chosen for him to view was dismal. Most were in the countryside with large gardens that would need to be tended and they all displayed a 'crumbling ruin' charm that would therefore require full restoration. In his view this made the low asking price completely irrelevant. I took him to one house that I adored. It hadn't been lived in since 1932 and had a dirt (pise) floor, no bathroom and an open fireplace for cooking. No kitchen as such and no electricity or toilet. I thought he would faint.

David insisted the agents show us only village houses that required little or no renovation. He wanted to be able to walk into a house that could be lived in immediately. He wanted to be able to stroll to the boulangerie and sit in the square having a coffee or a glass of wine. In truth so did I. I bowed to his more realistic judgement.

Over the following week we saw some pretty dreary little places that lacked charisma, to say the least. The houses we viewed were dark, depressing and icy cold inside because it was winter. Most smelt damp and some had been vacant for so long that they had been invaded by owls and pigeons. I was beginning to feel my dream unravelling.

Several days before our deadline to leave we were taken to see a house in a village very close to where I had been staying and very central to where all my new friends lived. The two-storey house was in the middle of the village, smack bang against a main road with pretty but peeling grey French front doors at the side. When we entered it was deathly dark but the agent quickly opened the four huge arched timber shutters covering the front of the house and winter sun streamed in, transforming the space. There was one big room downstairs that had a neat kitchen, a pine table and traditional timber dining chairs. There was a huge stone fireplace in the sitting room area with a black Godin wood stove and an add-on bathroom that was small but perfectly adequate. Two large and light bedrooms upstairs – the front room with a view to the village square and an impressive Romanesque church. I took David's hand as we wandered through.

What really clinched this property for me was that it had a leafy courtyard at the back plus an ancient stone barn with two original aged timber doors. A perfect space for sitting outside around a table in the summer.

We didn't discuss the pros and cons; David gave me a wink and I returned a big smile.

'We would like to put down a deposit,' he told the agent.

It was a mad rush completing the initial legalities and paperwork with just three days and we asked my good friend Claude, who lived just outside the village, if he would act as our proxy to sign the final contracts. The house would be ours in under three months.

We went back to take a second look the day before we left for Australia. It felt perfect. Houses always have a vibe and this one felt peaceful and positive to me. The big downstairs room was cold without the fire alight but I could really visualise myself here and I knew I could make it our own with just a few personal touches. It was meant to be.

15

Hoarding

One thing that continues to worry me during David's illness is the huge amount of 'stuff' we have accumulated over our decades together. One day I tentatively broach the subject of David's shed. When we moved to the farm he laid claim to the biggest and best insulated shed on the property. Fully lined with good lighting, it's where he stores all his office records and other paraphernalia that he's accumulated over his lifetime. We've only owned three houses in 43 years, each one larger than the previous one and with better storage, and so there's never been incentive to throw anything away or declutter when moving. Every new house was up-sizing! I've discarded lots of unwanted stuff over the decades – given our children furniture, linen, kitchen equipment, china, books, artworks. David, however, has systematically hung onto every single thing. He's a hoarder.

He's not the 'going to the tip and bringing home useless junk' type of hoarder. He's simply kept anything and everything that might be useful, or that had meant something at some stage. There's no rhyme or reason to his collection and certainly no method or order in the way it had been archived. 'Archived' is probably the wrong word. 'Stashed' is better.

When he closed up the little weatherboard cottage that had been his office for a decade in the mountains, he simply chucked everything into huge cardboard packing boxes. He emptied bookshelves and cupboards and drawers into these boxes, sealed them with masking tape and wrote in thick felt pen HANNAY'S OLD SHIT on every one. Which meant that he has no idea what's in any of the boxes and, to be honest, he's rarely ventured into that shed in the sixteen years we've been at Yetholme.

Many years before, when he closed up his big Sydney film production office, he contacted the Australian Film and Sound Archive to see if they had an interest in any of his filmic history. They certainly did, and an archivist spent a week rifling through cabinets and cupboards, meticulously itemising the records of numerous films David had produced over twenty-five years. They carefully transported sixteen large boxes of film paraphernalia to Canberra, and that took a huge burden of responsibility from David's shoulders.

What remained should probably have been discarded – given away or recycled, but it was all transported to the office in the mountains and eventually it all ended up at the farm. Plus much, much more that's been accumulated in the meantime.

When each film wraps up, David saves all the production office equipment. Phones, staplers, scissors, sticky tape, pens and pencils, reams and reams of paper – pink, white, blue, yellow. Obsolete typewriters and faxes, Polaroid cameras, recording devices, items of wardrobe, props. Anything that hasn't been sold off or redistributed by the various heads of departments.

It's madness, a mania, an obsession. There are dozens of filing cabinets still containing their files. Piles of magazines, newspapers and journals, and folder upon folder of financial records dating back decades.

Inside the house I've always been firm about not hoarding. David loves reading newspapers and hates throwing them out or letting me use them as mulch in the garden or to light a fire – unless every single article has been read. It's a fear of missing out on something. I return from my treks and tours to tall stacks of newspapers and weekend magazines on the bedroom chair and bedside tables. If I go to remove them there's be a gasp: 'I haven't finished reading those!' I have to use subtle tactics, removing the offending papers one at a time from the bottom of the stack until it's under control. David also loves to spread stuff out on surfaces so he can see them. Business papers, letters, bills, receipts, invoices. I allow him to cover every surface in the dining room four times a year while he's doing the quarterly books, but otherwise I help him file the papers away in his office. It's a constant struggle between us.

So, on the morning I tentatively mention the shed, David bristles.

'Don't you think it's time we sorted out what's in that shed? We've been meaning to do it for years, and it could be something quite good to do together,' I say gently.

'Harrumph.'

David simply doesn't know where to start and because he's feeling washed out and lacking in energy he's not at all motivated to launch into such a daunting project. Hoarders can't discriminate between what's worth keeping and what's of no further use.

This inability to make the decision about what should stay and what should go is the fundamental dilemma. I know, from cleaning up David's office once a year while he's at Cannes, that he's incapable of chucking stuff away. I've always been very respectful: sorting things into logical piles (film scripts, correspondence, financial records) but also making a huge pile of things that I believed should be discarded (doodle paper from beside the phone, shopping lists, old television programs and advertising leaflets left in the letterbox). I've never thrown one single thing away – just sorted it, dusted, polished the lovely old teak desk and had his office looking immaculate for his return.

He always scowls at what I've done, then enjoys spending the next twelve months layering a new collection of detritus on every surface.

We strike a deal. The shed contains at least 150 to 180 boxes as well as numerous filing cabinets and several overflowing shelving units. We'll bring just one box out of the shed every day, so we can sort through it together and 'deal with' the contents. Our sons put up additional metal shelving against the wall so that we can organise what's to remain in an orderly and accessible fashion.

This bit-by-bit approach is how I've always tackled garden maintenance – especially when I have been away for several months and everything is weedy and overgrown. I mentally divide the garden – no matter how large – into achievable squares. Maybe two metres square. I tackle the work slowly but surely, chipping away at the weeds, watering and mulching, and in a matter of weeks the entire garden is restored to order. If you look at it as a whole, it's overwhelming. If you break it down into achievable chunks, you'll get there in the end.

So the following day, after breakfast, I suggest bringing in ONE box – any box – from the shed for sorting.

'I can't today,' he responds. 'I have a long conference call and then I need to write a detailed email for the scriptwriter in London.'

Over the following days there's always a different pretext why the sorting out can't be started. 'I'm feeling like crap today'; 'I have to start on the books for the accountant'; 'I'm doing an oral history call from Melbourne'.

We never get to the shed. Not even one box. It sits there darkly, waiting for me to tackle later, at a moment in my life when I'm at my lowest, saddest ebb.

16

Happiness

In times of difficulty we turn to familiar comforts. I look around and think of the things in my life that bring me the most joy and pleasure, because I need them now.

Children loom large on the happiness scale – our grown-up kids but these days also our grandchildren. They bring such fresh joy and appreciation. There's no baggage, they just love you and are happy to hang around, laugh at your jokes and relish the food you cook for them (because you know what they like and you're not their parents). Being around and having the time for growing grandkids is satisfying, amusing and distracts me from life's troubles. David feels the same, to some extent. He loves mealtimes with the kids, going for walks and taking them to the movies. Especially taking them to the movies.

I organise for the children to come and stay as often as possible. They keep us real. There's no wallowing time when there's a houseful of kids. During the shorter school holidays they come for a week – over summer they come for three weeks. Sometimes two or three children. Anything up to seven or eight. This is my completely happy time, and I wonder if it buys into my 'excessive' tendencies.

When they stay for those long summer holidays I buy huge sacks of flour for making bread; rice in big calico bags and bulk potatoes. Literally truckloads of food. Boys outnumber girls in this next generation of ours, three girls and eight boys. Five teenage boys can eat a lot and they do. The holidays are punctuated by generous meals, including morning and afternoon teas. They spend most of their time outdoors and burn up a lot of energy which makes them even hungrier. During these visits I have no time for feeling sad, the kids have brought happiness with them.

Even when the children aren't around I still spend a lot of time cooking, as part of my ongoing mission to prevent David from losing any weight. Of course, this means I am also rounding out. A cooked lunch enjoyed with wine will do it for you. The time I've spent in France has corrupted my eating patterns and I love the concept that life should lead up to lunch as it does in rural villages. I focus on getting all my physical farm chores done first (mowing, slashing, watering the vegetables, feeding the animals, bringing in the firewood) and start preparing a meal just before midday, although I have been planning it since early morning.

David spends most of his mornings in his office talking with and emailing friends and colleagues. He's also started researching his family history, mainly through his mother's line. He seems to be able to go back a long way in this lineage and he finds himself connected with many famous (and infamous) people; it delights him. As the weeks and months pass he becomes a bit obsessive with this family tree and I realise how gratifying this must be for him. He's looking backwards instead of forwards. He shares his ancestral discoveries with his siblings and cousins and with me as well. I point out that his family were higher up the food chain than mine – I come from a long line of peasants. It's probably much easier to trace ancestors whose births, marriages, affairs and deaths were more prominently recorded.

By one o'clock it's time to sit down and relax together. I tell him what's going on around the farm; he tells me where he's up to with various projects and his online research. Conversation usually turns to politics – we're both a bit intense on that score. In all our forty-plus years together, we've never run out of things to say to each other. When we go to restaurants together we never look at our phones or gaze at the décor – we talk nonstop. Not that we always agree – far from it – but we thrive on the debate.

Sadly, one of the comforts that escapes me during this period is reading. I've always loved books, much more than television, and in the past I would spend most evenings tucked up with a book while David preferred to watch the box. I can still manage to read the weekend newspapers, but not lengthy or in-depth articles on complex issues. As for novels, I've virtually given up. My concentration seems shot to pieces and I find myself reading the same page or chapter several times. I just can't seem to follow the thread of a story and I get the characters confused. I'd love to escape into a cracking read, but I just can't sustain the interest. My other passion is music and this is not offering me much comfort either. Before we moved to the farm I used to catch the train to Sydney every few weeks for a symphony concert or recital. Most days I have classical music playing on a portable radio which I also take out into the garden. Now I am avoiding my musical favourites because they make me cry. I am irritated with myself for being so fragile.

After children, food, wine, music and books my pleasure comes from gardening. At various times of my life it has been my greatest single comfort – it's so easy to lose yourself in the garden. It's not something I do while thinking about something else; it's something that carries me away. I might just set off to do a bit of weeding in the vegetable garden but somehow this leads to turning over the soil and adding more compost, which in turns leads to trimming back trees and shrubs to allow in more sunlight – then the pruned leaves need shredding and adding to a new compost heap. And so it goes. When we lived in suburban Leura I would wander out in the morning, in my white cotton nightie, to pick up the morning newspaper. Two hours later David would come looking for me – I'd be filthy, having started gardening in bare feet and without gloves. He'd always remind me that, after all, I am a peasant.

For me gardening works as therapy on many levels. Physically I can exhaust myself spending a day outside, shovelling cow manure and wheeling the barrow up and down our sloping block of land. Squatting to weed is almost a yoga posture, as are the many twists, folds and bends that keeping the garden in order demands. I deliberately jump, feet together, the four stone steps that lead up and down to the vegetable patch – I do this several times a day as I carry stuff to the compost and when I nick up in the late afternoon to gather leafy greens for the evening meal – in the firm belief that the impact of my 'step jumps' is bone strengthening. There is nothing more life-affirming than digging a hole in the soil and planting a tree. The tree has a reason to live and grow; it has a future. It prompts me to look ahead instead of looking back. Meanwhile the clean air and the sun on my back have a healing effect and spending so much time outdoors keeps me in constant touch with the change of seasons. I feel part of it.

Gardening gently prods my brain into action. My ongoing curiosity about the life of plants engages me completely and I waste hours by googling individual varieties of trees, shrubs, perennials and roses and burying my head in plant catalogues to decide which combination of foliage and flower colours will work best in a particular corner or against a certain wall. The time then spent observing the growth and habits of these individual species is absorbing; in a sense like watching a child grow and change. I am fortunate indeed that my son and daughter-in-law (Ethan and Lynne) share these enthusiasms and we have many rambling conversations about the development of individual plants we have selected, taking ourselves on meandering garden tours to share our delight; taking close-ups of every new leaf, bud and flower for our ever-expanding plant photo album. It's pure joy.

Psychologically gardening has a powerful influence on my wellbeing. When I am simultaneously focussed and distracted it clears my head of worries and sadness. In the garden I forget what might be troubling me and escape the everyday realities of life. It's my way of letting go. Just me and the earth with the added pleasure of the creatures that share this space – from the birds above to the earthworms below. The chickens clucking and scratching around, the bees (both native and introduced) that are a constant and the snails and slaters that have now made their home along the rocky embankment at the back of the raised vegetable beds. I try not to view them as the enemy, but as part of the whole scheme of things – even the mice, rats and snakes that go with keeping poultry and making compost – are vaguely tolerated. I'm not trying to tame nature, to control the envi-ronment or to be in charge. I am satisfied to fit in and work with what's here, adding beauty and fascination every time a new seed is propagated or a row of seedlings is planted. Gardening teaches me patience and tolerance; it fosters curi-osity and wonder and ultimately allows me to surrender to aspects of the natural world that I cannot change. Being in the garden calls to something deep inside me. It has the same soothing effect on me as listening to good music.

Being in the garden connects me and at the same time it sets me free. The best thing I ever did was inadvertently stumbling upon this joy in my mid-twenties and it continues to sustain me now in my late sixties, at a point in my life that was impossible to imagine as a younger woman. Younger Mary could never have known how critical gardening would become; how I would grow to depend on it as a way of dealing with the anxiety and fear associated with caring for a very sick husband, and then afterwards helping to fill the very large empty space in my life.

17

Mercy dashes

There was a gap of six years between when Margaret was first diagnosed with Alzheimer's and David discovering he had cancer. During those years I spent a lot of time on Vancouver Island. Initially, in the early stages of the disease, Margaret's husband, Ken, was her primary carer, managing all the shopping, meals, medications and doctor visits. They had a weekly cleaner, which was a huge bonus, however he was obviously struggling with Margaret's personal care.

On reflection there had been many clues to Margaret's advancing dementia that I might have recognised if I'd allowed myself to imagine something so terrible. On that very first visit to the island we shared many memories and stories yet there were vast gaps in what she could recall. She had absolutely no memory, for example, of our cousins of a similar age to her, with whom she spent a huge amount of time both before and after the big trip to America. She had strong memories of the places where they had lived overseas but very little to say about the people they met: the school friends, the neighbours or her teachers. She was inclined to tell the same anecdotes over and over again. I didn't really notice until much later that her handwriting had been deteriorating every time she sent me a letter – I can see it clearly now. Her artwork also changed. Her painting style became fragmented, confused and more abstract. Perhaps if I'd been in contact with her over our entire lives I would have picked up on these changes. As she was 'new' to me, I just accepted her without question.

My initial angry response to her grim diagnosis also changed over time. I was intensely grateful to have found her when I did and not two years down the track when the possibility of all those marvellous conversations had vanished. I felt such enormous tenderness for her and her plight. She really, really didn't deserve this cruel outcome. Nobody does.

Each time I did a mercy dash to Vancouver Island there'd be lots of excitement, a celebratory dinner and visits from other family members. It would take me a few days to assess what was going on to determine how everything was being managed. By the time I visited in the middle of 2007 Margaret had become quite anxious and was incapable of sitting still for more than two minutes. It's a common stage of dementia, when the person realises they are losing cognitive function and distressingly struggles against it. I can't even begin to imagine Margaret's inner turmoil as she struggled to cling on to some semblance of control of her life. Although we still talked a lot and laughed together, most of our conversations were led by me and were becoming repetitive, the subjects narrowing down to just a few favourite themes.

Margaret was fixated on the calendar hanging on the kitchen wall, checking it every twenty minutes, needing to know the day, the date and any appointments that had been scribbled in as reminders. She was also obsessed with the two cats, letting them in and out constantly and topping up their food bowls twenty or thirty times a day.

Her hair desperately needed cutting and her nails needed trimming. Her clothes were in a mess – I sensed she'd been wearing the same two or three outfits over and over and not putting clothes out to be washed. I found the cats' food plates in her underwear drawer. It was time for me to tackle these issues and thankfully Ken was quite ready to admit he wasn't able to keep up with many aspects of her care. We discussed getting some home help, just for Margaret, and although initially reluctant at the thought of having a stranger in the house, he eventually agreed. Through a local nursing service we found a marvellous woman who lived nearby and who started coming over several afternoons a week to help with bathing, washing and preparing meals.

In the interim I needed to wrangle Margaret into a bath for a proper scrub and hair wash. The small guest bathroom had a manageable sized bath and I somehow helped her to strip her off and enticed her into the deep soapy water.

She immediately relaxed, just as irritable children do when plonked in a warm tub, and she allowed me to do her hair and scrub her gently all over. She smiled at me, saying, 'I do hope you have someone to do this for you at home. It feels lovely'. She was such a gentle person, always kind and concerned for others. I mourned her loss of memory and hoped that this sweet aspect of her personality would persist. I felt such fondness for her.

Margaret and Ken still attended the weekly art group, although she'd stopped wanting to paint. For a while she resisted going at all, saying she was embarrassed because she'd forgotten names. 'These are woman I've known for decades and I can't remember who they are,' she lamented. Once we'd arrived she seemed happier, although the restlessness and pacing was a constant. Ken loved these Wednesdays because of the generous lunch and the opportunity to chat with Margaret's oldest friends. As their contribution he'd picked up a barbecued chicken from the supermarket and everyone brought delicious homemade treats: soup, country breads, salads, pasta bakes and a myriad of sweet delights. Like Americans, the Canadians love their slices and every week there was an amazing new taste sensation. It was the culinary highlight of the week for Margaret and Ken when I wasn't around.

I also loved spending time with those feisty woman artists. They were intelligent, talkative and talented. They laughed a lot, but perhaps not as raucously as a similar group of Australian women would. Ken seemed a bit overwhelmed by them at times, and could rarely get a word in. Margaret couldn't stay long at the table; her agitated legs got her up and moving.

My ears pricked up when one of the women told me that her older sister had a fulltime, live-in carer from the Philippines. I later discovered it was a scheme supported by the Canadian government that allowed trained carers to be employed on a two-year contract to live in as carers of babies, young children and the elderly. If they remained employed for five years, they could apply for residency and then their families could join them, also as permanent residents. On the surface it seemed like a brilliant idea, and certainly one that could work for my sister. Ken was determined to keep Margaret at home until the end of her life, and even though I knew this was highly unusual with a disease like dementia, I believed it could be possible for a few years at least.

What worried me most was Ken's state of mind. He coped reasonably well as long as there were no hiccups – no unexpected complications – in their life. If a problem arose, even something as simple as a leaking tap or an issue with the car, he became irrationally upset. It was as though he was just barely hanging on, so easily rattled and flustered. It altered his personality, making him difficult to deal with. What I failed to notice were the multiple common symptoms of his undiagnosed Parkinson's disease. Depression, paranoia and delusions are all telltale signs that were not detected by me or any doctors, including the gerontologist they were seeing on a regular basis.

I was well aware that Ken spent a lot of time – almost all the time – alone with Margaret. They were no longer communicating conversationally – it was all about day-to-day tasks. This complete lack of mental stimulation and interaction with other people has devastating consequences for carers. I've read that a large percentage of people who have a partner with dementia also develop a neurological condition.

Up until this visit my focus had been only on Margaret and her evolving illness. Before leaving I started the ball rolling with an application for a fulltime Filipina carer, and could only hope that Ken and other family members would follow it through. I couldn't imagine Margaret being able to stay living at home, in these stressful conditions, until the end of her life. She was still pretty fit – small and wiry with lots of energy. She could easily live another five years, or even more.

When I boarded the small plane from the island to Vancouver, it was with mixed feelings of anxiety and relief. I worried about how things would go until a fulltime carer can be found; a process that might take more than six months. But I knew I'd be back before then.

18

Getting on with things

At the front of our property is a small creek with a bridge we drive over to get up to the farmhouse and paddocks. Known locally as Frying Pan Creek, it's a tributary of the larger Fish River, a permanent stream feeding the Murray–Darling Basin. As one of the state's most important waterways there are schemes to conserve the flow and improve the water quality, which includes the smaller tributaries like ours. When we first moved to the farm, our creek was thickly overrun by willow trees, which look pretty in a traditional English way but which are slowly strangling the natural water flow.

Older locals describe to me how the creek looked when they were kids, edged by local gums and wattles and full of birds and wildlife, including platypus. We gradually start removing the willows and then are approached by a water catchment group who are encouraging lots of local farmers to do the same, and to replant with indigenous plant species. It's called the Fish River project and a few months before David's diagnosis I sign up to work with environmental experts on restoring the health of the creek.

Owning land, even a small patch like our twenty-five acres, is a big responsibility. There's a natural spring in the middle of the farm that overflows into a wetland where native reeds and rushes grow in abundance. The water from this goes down to Frying Pan Creek so it's vital that all three water systems remain unpolluted. From the kitchen window we can see birds flocking to the wetlands, tracks where wombats stomp through at night, and the ever-present swamp wallabies. We consider ourselves so fortunate to have such beauty around us.

Two of our sons have trained in horticulture and are expert at controlling weed infestations like the rogue willows. On weekend visits they help us to slowly remove the problem trees. I've been given a list of suitable replacement trees, shrubs and reeds that are local to the region. It's a much-needed diversion for me, getting involved in a project this worthwhile which also gets me out of the house and into nature. I phone up local nurseries and bush regeneration groups to find the plants I need.

When the grandchildren visit the farm they spend a lot of time hanging out at the creek, climbing the willows and getting themselves wet and muddy. I'm aware they will miss these trees, but there are so many other wooded areas on the

My parents Muriel Angel and Theo Moody in a classic 1940s street photograph taken in Sydney. They met while both working in the *Daily Telegraph* newsroom.

During WWII my father was posted to New York as a foreign correspondent and Muriel, with the children from his first marriage, joined him six months later. They were living the high life but their marriage was already in trouble.

As a young cadet journalist at the *Australian Women's Weekly* a fashion photographer persuaded me to pose for this studio shoot. Not long after this snap was taken, he inveigled me into taking my clothes off for the rest of the session. I was obviously not very worldly.

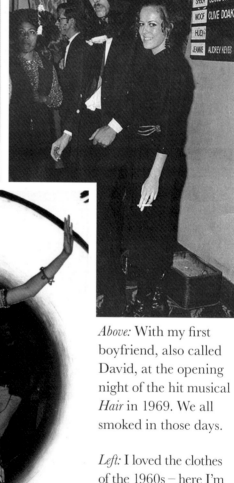

Above: With my first boyfriend, also called David, at the opening night of the hit musical *Hair* in 1969. We all smoked in those days.

Left: I loved the clothes of the 1960s – here I'm at Luna Park, on one of the rides, while covering the Sydney University Ball for the 'People and Fashion' pages of the magazine.

The day we carried our firstborn Miriam home from hospital, outside our little sandstock cottage in Crows Nest. This picture was taken by one of the TV directors we worked with at Channel 9, hence the theatrical pose.

David's 45th birthday party in 1984 where we dressed as a bride and groom just for a lark – we didn't actually officially marry for another ten years.

Off to a fancy dress party – I dressed David as a garden gnome (typecasting), myself as my heroine Dame Edna Everage and Mum wore her pink pyjamas and a turban.

Not long before we left Sydney for the Blue Mountains, David bought himself a 1949 Mark V Jaguar – an unexpected extravagance for a man usually prudent with money. The car is still in the family.

In my early forties I started work as the NSW presenter on the ABC's *Gardening Australia* program. We filmed segments every three weeks and wrote extensively for the popular monthly magazine.

The film crews travelled from Hobart to record segments. Here we are putting together a series of episodes on the extensive landscaping for the 2000 Sydney Olympic Games complex.

Our happy years at the Leura house where my mother Muriel lived with us until she died. David's son Tony also came to live with us during this period, creating a big extended and blended family.

We added rooms to the house to accommodate the size of our family. Getting a bear hug from David in our renovated kitchen.

I was astonished to become a grandmother in my early forties – here with the three oldest boys Sam, Hamish and Eamonn.

The pretty backdoor garden at the farm near Bathurst we bought in 2000. The cold climate was a challenge – Yetholme is where the Great Western Highway is closed several times a year due to heavy snow.

We inherited a large flock of geese when we bought the farm. I loved having the space for so many animals – including ducks, chickens, goats, sheep and alpacas.

The garden at Yetholme was glorious with established trees and rhododendrons. I added lots of colourful annuals and perennials.

The farm was 'the happy place' for our grandchildren as they grew up.
I encouraged them to run wild and Isabella (in her wheelchair) was never
far from the action.

David mellowed over the decades and was more calm with our grandkids than
with our own children. Here he's multi-tasking with Owynn on his lap.

Heading off for a long walk around the farm. Often we carried a picnic lunch and disappeared for hours.

I took Eamonn (centre back) and Sam (front row right) trekking in Nepal with a group of other grandmothers and their grandkids. It was an amazing experience for all of us.

A fun photo taken at the farm by our French photographer friend Nadja La Ganza. She wanted us to dress up so I wore my wedding dress and a hat bought in India. David in his dressing gown and a panama hat.

Early days on the front porch of the Yetholme farmhouse with our placid Labrador, Luscious.

Our small house (on the right with grey shutters) in the village of Frayssinet-le-Gélat in southwest France. The church is Romanesque and the bells ring every hour and half hour, twenty-four hours a day.

It's a bright and sunny house with just one big room downstairs, looking out to the village.

We put in a new but very simple kitchen. There are weekly markets in nearby villages where I shop for fresh ingredients most days – in the French tradition.

The creamy old stone smothered in a Himalayan Musk rose. There's not much space for a garden so I plant out hanging baskets of flowers in the summer.

Buying baguettes for a picnic lunch with one of my tour groups. For years I have led gourmet walking tours in the region near our house, visiting some of the best gardens and restaurants.

In winter the house is cosy with its thick stone walls and a log fire. The glass doors lead to a small courtyard garden and an old barn.

My first meeting with my long lost sister Margaret, who I tracked down on Vancouver Island in Canada after the publication of my first memoir *Au Revoir*. I couldn't believe how alike we were in spite of being separated for nearly fifty years.

In her late sixties Margaret developed Alzheimer's disease and I went back and forth to Canada to help with her care over a period of nine years. Here we are with her much loved live-in carer Fedema Sapalo.

My career as a tour guide became busier and more demanding in my fifties. I often went directly from a trek over to Vancouver Island to spend time with Margaret before returning home.

With a yoga trekking group in Ladakh on the Tibetan and Kashmir borders in northern India. I seem irresistibly attracted to remote regions.

The snowy road leading to the Nubra Valley in Ladakh. The air is very thin so we didn't hang around for long.

The twin goats I helped deliver while reading step by step instructions on a YouTube clip. They became my special babies.

Our children at David's last birthday celebration at the farm (from left) Tony, Miriam, Aaron and Ethan. They supported us through the toughest of times.

David looking so healthy and happy during his eleven month 'remission'. I treasure this image captured by my cousin Marcelle's husband Royce Holiday.

The last Christmas photograph of us with our eleven gorgeous grandchildren ranging in age from four months to 20 years. Eight boys, three girls. Looking at the photograph now, I can clearly see how gravely ill David looks.

The final farewell at the old Yetholme cemetery. Lowering the casket handmade by Ethan into the grave dug by Aaron. A DIY funeral.

I still can't quite work out how to do a selfie. In my bedroom in Blackheath with David's portrait.

Painted by Qui Ming this intense depiction of David captures a powerful aspect of his character. It's a comfort to me.

My new space in the family home I share with Ethan, Lynne and their children. Downsizing to this extent forced me to keep only those things that are most precious to me.

One edge of the garden has a beautiful old drystone wall, which is a perfect backdrop for the new garden beds.

The vegetable garden and chook house at Blackheath. I love working in raised beds and the chickens are let out to scratch in the orchard at the rear of their enclosure.

The garden beds at the front of the house have come together very quickly, under the shade of the old Maple tree. Creating this garden with Ethan and Lynne has been great therapy.

In the Sahara with one of my Morocco tour groups. It was a new horizon for me.

A need to try a completely new destination led me to Morocco five years ago. I instinctively knew I needed different challenges.

The Himalayas have become a powerful part of my life. They keep drawing me back.

Above: Prayer flags against a perfect mountain sky. My 'other' home.

Left: I feel fitter today than when I first started trekking nearly thirty years ago.

property where they can play, and I will include them in the good environmental message around why the creek must be cleared and replanted.

One of the main social changes I've observed during my lifetime is the comparatively small amount of time children spend outdoors, just mucking about playing and getting into mischief. It saddens me to realise this trend is universal, with an entire generation – our grandkids' generation – spending so many of their leisure hours indoors connected to a device rather than outside using their imaginations in some shared game. David and I often talk about our childhood adventures, being part of an era where children were virtually ejected from their homes after breakfast during school holidays and at the weekends. Our parents had little or no idea where we went to play – in my case to the beach; in David's down a streambank and into the New Zealand bush. We came home for lunch and were shooed out again until just before dinner time. Apart from reading a book or playing a board game there was not much happening inside the house, and parents believed that bored children were nothing but trouble. They made a mess and got into fights. Much better outside and out of sight.

Our children's generation were also 'outsiders', maybe not as strictly evicted, but certainly encouraged to not hang around the house. I was quite tough about television viewing times – one hour per day during the school week and only a couple of hours on weekend mornings. It was the only chance David and I had to stay in bed a little longer. Bliss. During school holidays I wouldn't let my kids watch television unless the weather was absolutely frightful – raining or snowing.

I've continued this regime when the grandchildren come to the farm, and they've never really complained. They are always so happy to see each other – siblings from three families who only get together during these extended farm holidays. They break up into smaller groups, or gangs, and disappear for hours at a time. I only hear from them if someone trips over a snake or has an injury. Quickly patched up, I send them out again. We also go for long walks together – or David takes them off for hours. By the end of the day they'd be starving hungry and worn out. Perfect.

We've been so fortunate to have the space to offer the kids an opportunity to run wild. These days, outdoor recreation for children seems to be structured and supervised, and this doesn't build resilience or independence. I really hope there's a big swing back to reconnecting our children to the natural world; to allowing them the space to explore and experience life away from the anxious gaze of a parent. David describes it very well when he tells me that he and his playmates had an entire world of shared adventures and games of imagination that their parents knew nothing about. The secret life of children. He loved the idea that his parents were no part of that world. It made it even more special. I've never thought of it that way, but when he voices that feeling I immediately connect. I wonder if modern parents would be happy with their children having an 'other' life without them.

19

Help arrives at last

Neither my sister nor her husband understood anything about computers, so communication between us depended upon letter writing and telephone calls. Margaret had been a regular letter writer, but when she was no longer capable of corresponding we relied on the phone for keeping in touch. Ken wasn't much of a talker, so I didn't phone just for a chat and he only called if he had something important or worrying to say.

In a sense, when I wasn't with them at the farm on Vancouver Island, it all seemed like a dream. My sister on the other side of the world progressively slipping into a different headspace. Her husband also gradually losing the plot and becoming trickier to manage. When Ken called me out of the blue in July 2008 I was tugged back into their world.

I'd just returned from a tour in the Indian Himalayas and was not quite back in the 'real world'.

'We have the Filipina carer coming in three weeks,' he told me. 'Can you come and meet her please?' He offered to pay my fares, which was kind. This was several years before David's diagnosis and he'd just returned from the Cannes Festival. We hadn't spent any time together for more than six weeks but, as ever, he was totally supportive of my decision to pack my bags yet again, and head for Canada.

When Margaret and I found each other again, after nearly fifty years of separation, nobody could have been more delighted than David. He'd become part of the story, having listened to me talk about my sense of sister-loss since we first got together more than thirty-five years before. I wasn't obsessively lamenting this rift in the family, just wistfully fantasising about how lovely it would be if I could find Margaret. When I did reconnect with her he was thrilled to bits, and continued to applaud my decision to spend as much time as possible with her, especially once she was ailing.

It was a huge relief knowing that finally Ken and Margaret would have a fulltime live-in carer, and I arrived two days before she was due to fly in from Manila, and helped organise a comfortable and welcoming bedroom for her. It was a large and sunny room with enough space for her own lounge chair, television and desk. She would be sharing the spare bathroom with me, but only during the times I come to lend a hand.

In the late afternoon she arrived with the Filipina woman who organised all these international 'placements'. Her name was Fedema Sapalo and she seemed very nervous and shy. It wasn't yet winter but quite cold and grey. Coming from the Philippines, the weather must have been bit of a shock – the whole situation would have been a huge adjustment for her.

I stayed for three weeks to show Fedema the ropes and support her. She spoke perfect English and had a charming sense of humour.

I kept preparing the meals, writing down the recipes so that Fedema could cook the food Margaret and Ken liked – by the end of day one I'd discovered that she'd never cooked Western-style meals, let alone eaten them. After the fragrant and spicy cuisine of home, my food must have tasted bland and stodgy to her. I hoped she could introduce some Asian food into Ken and Margaret's diet, for her own sake apart from anything else.

Fedema and Margaret quickly bonded. She had a soft voice, and constantly chatted to Margaret while helping her to bathe, dress and eat. She sat next to Margaret, gently stroking her arm, took her for a walk twice a day, made sure she drank plenty of water. I had a strong sense that it was all going to work out.

At night we cleaned up the kitchen together while Margaret and Ken watched television and I learned about Fedema's situation. She'd just spent twelve months caring for an elderly woman in Hong Kong – this was a requirement for her to be eligible for the temporary Canadian visa. She needed at least a year's work experience to qualify for this job. She'd only been back with her family – her husband and four children aged four to ten – for a week when the call came to take up the job on Vancouver Island.

I was shaken by the realisation that our desire to keep Margaret in her own comfortable home in a wealthy first-world country directly caused heartbreaking family separation in a less fortunate part of the world. I didn't feel comfortable with this concept and yet was trapped by a decision that was made with the best of intentions. There's a strong argument that giving these hard-working women an opportunity to escape from the poverty of their own countries, where there is not enough work and bleak futures for their children, is a benevolent gesture. I couldn't see it this way. All I saw was the pain of young children separated from their mother; the conflict of the mother who must leave her family behind to try and carve a future for them all on the other side of the world. It was devastating.

Emailing back and forth with David, I shared my reservations about the ethics of the situation. He was more aware of the spread of Filipina women working in these situations than I, having lived for months at a time making films in cities like London, Rome and New York where many of Fedema's countrywomen have been employed as carers and housekeepers for decades. He'd also worked in Manila and pointed out that the country's largest export is its own people – both men and women, away from their families for months and even years at a time. I was deeply conflicted.

Fedema was well educated and qualified as a bookkeeper/accountant but she wasn't able to find any viable work at home. Over the next three weeks we established a great rapport. We talked about our families and I showed her photographs of my grandchildren, some of them about the same age as her kids. It was clear she was still quite culture-shocked as we compared our very different lifestyles. She was warm, open and talkative.

Ken had signed a two-year contract. Fedema worked six days a week, with Sundays free. I drove her up to the bus stop – the farm was quite a walk from the local township – and she would spend the day meeting with other carers in the same position as her. They would go to church, then head into the city to have lunch and wander around the shopping malls. She was entitled to two weeks annual leave but because she sent money home every fortnight, would not have enough to pay her return airfares.

Before I left, I had a serious talk with Ken. I could see he was very happy with Fedema and that her presence in the home greatly improved their quality of life. I told him to ensure she got home to her family every year – for three weeks at the very least. I committed to take over the carer's role during these 'holidays'. He agreed and also to paying Fedema's airfares. This was the only way I could accept the position we were in.

I kept visiting two or three times a year, including the times when Fedema made her annual trip back to the Philippines. Increasingly I needed an extra person to help me during these visits, as Margaret became progressively more difficult to manage alone. Eventually she couldn't walk unassisted, yet Ken insisted she kept having quite long walks outside every day, to maintain her mobility. I agreed in principle but worried that he was becoming more and more controlling about Margaret's care and how the household was managed. He had major fallings-out with various family members and imagined that visitors or part-time carers were stealing things. Fedema kept everything together, somehow tolerating Ken's erratic, irrational behaviour. When I visited she told me how volatile he could be, shouting at her and other carers. Shouting at Margaret. And yet, she said, at other times he was as sweet as a lamb – kind, generous and grateful for her care.

It took years, however, before he was finally diagnosed with Parkinson's disease. He denied the diagnosis and became angrier and more cantankerous as his life became more restricted. The medication helped a little but when his driver's licence was removed it placed them in a really difficult situation, stranded out on the farm and not able to drive to the shopping centre. Family members helped. It was precarious, but at least Fedema and I were able to keep in touch via email and she updated me on a regular basis. I worried about how she'd continue to cope and that worry intensified when David was diagnosed with cancer. My priority as a carer was at home, and I couldn't see myself being able to just jump on a plane and dash to Vancouver Island any time soon. I had to resist my strong 'rescuing' tendencies.

20

Reflections

Is it genetic inheritance or the circumstances of our lives that makes us who we are? Before becoming a mother I held strong views that environment was more fundamental in forming character than genetic inheritance. Later, as I observed our children grow in their totally different and often contradictory ways, I started to see that what they brought with them at birth was more important than anything I did (or didn't do) for them or with them. This belief was confirmed even later by my observation of our eleven grandchildren, who carry a varied array of physical genetic similarities, although they are complete individuals – so utterly different from each other it's laughable.

Yet I do acknowledge that major life events can hugely alter the development and behaviour of individuals. My parents, for example, were profoundly influenced by the First World War followed by the Great Depression. It informed them socially and politically, and they carried the beliefs they formed during these monumental world events to their graves.

David's childhood was disrupted by the Second World War and its aftermath. His father was an attractive but volatile man; his mother beautiful, intelligent but emotionally fragile. They were both creatives working in theatre and radio and David carried all of these inherited genes and inclinations. He could be explosive but was also highly sensitive. He was compassionate, very loyal but also very anxious. Mostly about money and failure. Decades ago, David was persuaded to enrol in a slightly wacky 'self-realisation' workshop suggested by a colleague. He had always described himself as an 'angry man', which he ascribed to his father's rejection of him when he returned from the war a damaged individual. David came home after this two-day intensive brainwashing session minus his beard and long hair, wearing a suit and tie. I was bemused. He suddenly described himself as 'powerful and loving' which to me was just a load of silly psychobabble. He was indeed powerful and very loving and always had been. As well as being angry and anxious, yet kind and genuinely interested in and supportive of people he worked with. He was far too complex to label in just one quirky catchphrase.

I'm sure that back when I was going through high school there must have been kids with dyslexia or Asperger's syndrome or attention deficit disorder or insipient bipolar disorder. They were never given a diagnosis or a label. Some of my schoolmates were exuberant extroverts; some withdrawn introverts. Some naturally cheerful and optimistic; some gloomy and negative.

When we had our one and only school reunion twenty years after finishing high school – when we were in our late thirties – it was fascinating how everyone seemed basically the same as they had been in their teens. The happy ones seemed bubbly; the cheerless ones still gloomy. Regardless of the circumstances of their lives – married, single, divorced, gay, career successful, with or without children – they appeared to me to have sustained their inborn personalities. Was it innate? Or had these deep-seated character traits been formed in early childhood, before I had known them?

I have gradually understood that some of my adult behaviours are learned responses to my childhood environment. As the daughter of an argumentative, alcoholic couple, very early in my life I developed strategies that I hoped might help soften the situation, that would make day-to-day life smoother, more tolerable. I was very helpful around the house, picking up on some of the chores my mother would have done before she went back to work when I was seven. Setting and clearing the table; putting away the groceries that were delivered in cardboard boxes by the back door; peeling the vegetables for dinner. Mum would be tired and irritable when she got home and so my getting these chores done brightened her mood considerably. I also felt needed. Valued.

My first boyfriend was a bit of a mess when I met him. Expelled from a private school, he landed at our public high school with long hair, a dope-smoking habit and a negative attitude. When I got my first job and a reasonable salary we moved in together in a share house. I earned the money for the rent, did the shopping, the cooking, the cleaning. I'm not sure what he did all day, but he never found work. I was rescuing him, and again it made me feel needed.

When I met David he was in a state of flux. Separated from his pregnant wife, he had recently broken up with his girlfriend and was heartbroken and depressed. From my perspective he was a much safer option than boyfriend number one. He had a good job in television, a smart car and a groovy little apartment. I thought he was rescuing me, but the reverse was to happen. All his friends said I'd turned his life around. That they'd never seen him so happy. I felt needed.

When David's show got cancelled, I had to wean our baby at six weeks and get my old job back. I certainly felt very needed indeed.

This pattern has continued through my adult life. At various times I've rescued my mother, one of my brothers, in some senses my sister and also one of my sons. I'm not convinced being a rescuer is the healthiest option for me, or anyone really, but I figure it's so ingrained in my psyche now that I'll be repeating this pattern until the day I die.

21

Ups and downs

THE FARM, 2012

The chemotherapy continues, with David spending a full day at the clinic every three weeks. During this treatment he deteriorates physically but seems to grow stronger mentally, having had some time to adjust to his predicament. The human spirit is remarkable. All the fear, anger, negativity and denial has been overtaken by a drive to stay alive for as long as possible. Those worrying emotions still exist, buried somewhere below the surface, but he has managed to find an appreciation of his life just as it is. For me, it's a huge relief.

Friends and family are a constant. Childhood pals from his days in New Zealand, a cousin and her husband we haven't seen for years, actors, writers, directors, composers, comedians . . . So many celebratory lunches and dinners, wonderful memories are stirred up and thrashed over. It's a nonstop party.

He really needs to stay connected to his work colleagues, and a staunch band of long-term film industry friends stay in regular communication. Emails, phone calls and visits. They also come for lunch, and David is more vocal, opinionated and expansive than ever. One Melbourne filmmaking friend has been doing a recorded oral history with him, over the phone. Once a week he sits up in bed with coffee and the newspapers, talking for hours. In every sense these conversations are helping him unpack his life, to make sense of it. I'm well aware that my own writing is a form of therapy, helping me to gain insight and understanding into the events of my life. In the same way David tells anecdotes and stories that bring back memories and emotions, both good and bad.

And yet, we still don't talk about death except in a cavalier or dismissive way. We don't seem capable of having that fundamental conversation about the inevitability of dying. We are clinging to the notion that there's still plenty of time. I'm not sure whether this procrastination is avoidance or a reluctance to put our fears into words. When I do, very rarely, think about David dying it's always a slow, drawn out process. I imagine myself sitting at his bedside, holding his hand, talking calmly and telling him I love him. Even inside my own head I refuse to project myself forward to that time when I will be alone. It seems disloyal – a betrayal – to visualise a world without him. I refuse to do it. We are living in the present and coping the best we can.

Every now and again David's anger or fear will bubble up. He's resentful about having missed this year's Cannes

Festival and gets frustrated when he reads about it in various film journals. If a prominent person dies, especially 'after a long battle with cancer', he feels it keenly. He's concerned about pain management at the end of his life, although he doesn't ask questions about it during medical visits. It just niggles away at him. Several times he mumbles bitterly 'the best thing that could happen would be to crash my car into a tree on the way into town'. I brush these melodramatic mutterings aside, reminding him that he'd probably end in hospital with hideous injuries as well as cancer. Obviously, neither of us is coming to grips with the future.

Then everything changes. Chemo finishes and almost immediately David starts to regain a sense of wellbeing. His skin colour brightens, his hair and beard rapidly regrow and the metallic taste in his mouth fades away. Energy returns and he's sleeping much better and laughing a lot. We live in this state of buoyant limbo for five or six weeks while waiting to have a follow-up full body scan to measure the effectiveness of the chemo treatment. We resume going to a movie once or twice a week, a pleasure we'd had to forgo as he'd been too unwell to enjoy it, and have lunch in town. Our combined sense of relief is palpable, having survived two gruelling rounds of medical intervention.

The oncologist is delighted with the test results and tells us that the primary tumour in the oesophagus is, to all intents and purposes, no longer apparent. He adds that the 'hot spots' that indicated the spread of the cancer cells have also been knocked right back by the chemo. He isn't saying that the cancer has gone, he's saying that it has taken a severe beating.

Medically, the word 'remission' is only applied to patients who have been cancer-free for five years. What we are offered is a 'period of remission' while the body recovers strength after the assault of the therapy. Hopefully then the return of the cancer will be very, very slow. David feel positive and believes that the burst of life and energy he's experiencing reflects the effectiveness of the treatment. To him the benefit of what's been happening internally is now apparent externally.

We excitedly phone everyone with our good news and we celebrate, just the two of us. The toxic drugs are now well out of his system and we can pick up the threads of our lives and our relationship. Making love in the mornings, it feels weirdly as though nothing has happened. It must have been a bad dream. I feel safe again; I start planning a trek in the Himalayas for next year and David returns to working on his beloved film projects.

Then, five days after the euphoria of our good news, everything changes yet again. Ken phones to say that Margaret has been overwhelmed by a massive infection from an ulcer on her lower back. She's dying. I pack my bags and leave the following afternoon for Vancouver Island.

22

Goodbye Margaret

VANCOUVER ISLAND, NOVEMBER 2012

Over the past few years the journey to Canada has become much less stressful due to the introduction of a direct flight from Sydney to Vancouver. Just twelve hours instead of the eighteen hours-plus route via Los Angeles, with two more flights to reach the island. I'm frightened I won't get there in time.

It's just over a year since I've seen my sister, but Fedema and I have been in touch regularly and I have an understanding about how they're all managing. We've kept this communication hush-hush from Ken, who feels threatened if he's not in the loop. Effectively, Fedema is now caring for two people, although I'm relieved to learn that there have been several extra carers employed to help her manage the workload. Fedema has delayed visiting her children and mother back in the Philippines because of Margaret's deteriorating condition. The startling decline in Margaret's condition has taken them all by surprise. What began as a small bedsore quickly developed into a massive, deep ulcer. Margaret hasn't managed to eat anything for almost a week and has had minimal fluids. Via email, Fedema has warned me that Margaret hasn't communicated in any way for months, so I'm prepared. At least, I think I am.

I'm picked up at the airport by one of Ken's relatives. It's early evening and I enter the house from the garage, through the kitchen. I'm talking as I walk through the back door and am astonished to see Margaret, not in her hospital bed, but propped up in a recliner chair in front of the television. She hears my voice, turns her head and actually smiles, though her eyes are glazed and watery. Later Fedema tells me it's the first time Margaret has responded to any voice for many months.

Ken is also in a recliner chair and he tries his best to get up, but I can see he's struggling. I can't believe how frail and unsteady on his feet he's become since I last saw him.

There are two extra carers and Fedema has been cooking dinner for everyone. I'm amused to see it's one of the recipes I taught her when she first arrived. We eat together around the kitchen table and Margaret remains fidgeting in her chair which has been pointed in the direction of some mindless quiz program. We transfer her back to the bedroom and this gives me a chance to talk alone to Fedema. It's a disturbing conversation.

Margaret is now the responsibility of the local palliative care team. A port has been inserted into her thigh for the regular administration of morphine due to the severity of the ulcer, and a nurse comes every morning to check her, change the dressing and help Fedema give her a wash and a fresh nightdress. She is allowed up to four doses of the painkilling drug per twenty-four hours. However, tearfully, Fedema tells me that Ken has forbidden the use of morphine except for just one daily dose, to be given an hour before the morning nurse arrives.

I look at the medication logbook provided by the team and see just one entry a day. Margaret cannot speak and she sleeps a lot. However, when she's awake she looks agitated and wild-eyed. It must surely be the pain.

A hospital bed has been installed for Ken in the main bedroom, which resembles a hospital ward. There's a table for the medications, piles of dressings, clean changes of linen and pillows so that Margaret's position can be routinely changed. However once Margaret is put to bed at night Fedema doesn't see her again until the following morning, so she has no idea if she's comfortable or in pain during the night. This means she's lying in exactly the same position for ten hours, which must surely impact on the ulcer.

I sit with Ken for a while, and he tells me, quite sadly, that when his mother died two decades ago it was within minutes of being given a shot of morphine. He's therefore convinced that Margaret will die from being overdosed with painkillers. I understand his fears, but I am also perturbed by the thought that Margaret is suffering needlessly. That night I sleep in my old room, the spare room where I have slept so often over the last seven years. I'm exhausted from the journey but I wake in the early hours, worrying how Margaret is faring; concerned that she could be awake and miserable.

On my laptop I've done some reading about people with Alzheimer's and their perception of pain. In the later stages of the disease, when sufferers are unable to really communicate, it's very challenging to determine if they are feeling intense pain or not. In the earlier stages, there's a belief that Alzheimer's somehow intensifies the sufferer's perception of pain, but again this theory is debatable. I remember vividly a few years ago Margaret had a fall in the middle of the night and didn't wake anyone. She simply went back to bed and went back to sleep. In the morning when we woke her and went to help her get up, it was obvious that she was injured and this was quickly confirmed by an X-ray that showed a fracture to her left forearm. Ken vaguely remembered hearing her fall, but when she took herself back to bed he simply assumed she was fine.

So, did she feel any pain and have no way of expressing it or of asking for help? Or was she oblivious to the pain of a fractured arm? At that time, apart from keeping the injured limb immobilised, we treated her with paracetamol and anti-inflammatories for at least ten days after the accident, assuming she would otherwise be uncomfortable.

The morning after I arrive we prepare Margaret for the visit from the nurse. She is looking relaxed, having been given her small dose of morphine, and I stay while the dressing is changed. The ulcer is horrendous but Margaret appears unfussed. Ken is hovering, but I still manage to have a few quiet moments to question the nurse about pain relief. She checks the logbook and the prescription, and reassures me that the doses are quite small, designed just to keep Margaret peaceful. For me, the word 'peaceful' is the key. Without pain relief she has a rigid, slightly startled facial expression. After the morphine she is serene. She deserves serenity.

I know that I'll get nowhere trying to reason with Ken so I decide to use my own common sense and initiative, following precisely the guidelines given by the palliative team. At least Ken has stopped demanding that Margaret be taken for her twice-daily walk – she can't even totter three steps without two people supporting her. It's now essential to lift her, which causes visible distress, and Fedema has stopped trying to take her to the toilet – she keeps her beautifully clean with sponge baths and routine checking.

In the late afternoon Ken again wants Margaret to be brought out to the sitting room, to watch television beside him. She has been given only one dose of pain relief since early morning and her face appears anguished during the transfer. I can understand how Ken believes that Margaret will just die if left on her bed, day and night. He believes she needs to be out where things are happening – the meal is being prepared and there is a fire burning in the hearth. However, I have a strong gut feeling that Margaret is not benefiting from this evening routine, which has been going on ever since her condition began to deteriorate. Before that, she was still up and dressed until bedtime.

Seeing Margaret lying awkwardly on the vinyl recliner, her face contorted and the sound level of the quiz show blaring across the room, causes something in me to snap. I burst into tears and tell Fedema and the other carer to gently take Margaret back to her bed. When Ken objects, to my shame, I shout at him: 'Can't you see Margaret is dying and she is obviously in pain? She needs to be given her morphine and kept comfortable and safe in her bed. One of us will stay with her all the time, twenty-four hours a day. She will never be alone. She's at the end of her life and she needs peace. I will not let my sister die stuck in front of that hideous quiz show!'

Margaret is not near enough to hear my outburst. I run from the room. Poor Ken, sitting in his chair, stunned. I give Margaret her evening dose of morphine and write it up in the logbook. I sit with her while the others have dinner, and Fedema sits with her while I have mine and clean up the kitchen. I then move her recliner chair from the sitting room into the bedroom so that I can sleep beside her. I set myself up for the night – a pillow, a blanket, a book and a torch. I will be her night nurse.

Nothing is ever said about my outburst. Ken just accepts that I've seized the reins and is very sweet to me and to the other carers. It reminds me a bit of my father, who was a classic bully unless challenged. Then he'd back off and behave like a lamb. I am so upset to feel that I have 'won the day'. For me it's a hollow victory because it's not about my taking control; it's about staying close to Margaret, monitoring her and making sure she has pain relief if she becomes conscious or restless during the night. It is all I can do.

When I dwell on the people in my life who have died, and how I feel about and have been affected by those deaths, I face myriad emotions.

My younger sister Jane died in infancy when I was not quite three years old. I have no tangible memory of Jane as a baby but I do recall clearly seeing my mother, reed thin, walking home down the steep hill to our block of flats after visiting her in the children's hospital. I must have known Mum was expected home and I was waiting, sitting on the low brick front fence at the front of our block of flats. I can remember her prominent cheekbones and the dark circles under her eyes.

The implications of Jane's death were profound for my brother and me. Our kindly neighbour drove us to her sister's farm at Taralga, near Goulburn. I guess we'd been told that Jane had died and we were being sent away on a holiday. If we were traumatised by being suddenly separated from our parents for the first time, I don't remember. My memories of our time at this farm are lovely. Our hostess was a middle-aged single woman (although we thought she was terribly old) caring for her elderly father, who was still running the farm. She was quite wonderful to us. She cooked lovely meals, she included us in all the farm activities such as shearing and feeding the orphan lambs, and tucked us warmly into bed at night. She took us to the little Anglican church on the hill on Sunday mornings – an absolute novelty for the children of atheists. I loved it.

After about six or eight weeks Mum came down on the train to take us home. From that time, for many years afterwards, we returned to the farm for school holidays once a year. These memories are all happy for me, but I do wonder if that first unexpected separation from our mother caused us emotional problems.

In my teens a male friend was killed in a car accident. At that age the possibility of death is seldom contemplated, so my emotions were more about shock and disbelief than grief. I remember thinking about all he had lost – his future life had vanished. I don't think I really had my head around it.

When I was twenty-two my father died by his own hand. I was pregnant with my first child and I recall feeling shock but not sorrow. My father's health had deteriorated after decades of hard drinking and chain smoking. His relationship with my mother had become toxic and he'd moved out of the family home into a small dingy flat where he ended his life. My mother had been tormented by his philandering, drinking and abusive temper, yet unbelievably (to me) she still loved him. I felt an overwhelming sense of relief and release at his death, hopeful that my mother might now go on to build a life of her own. I didn't feel anger, or sadness or grief. I was glad it was over.

In my thirties, my first boyfriend who I'd lived with for a couple of years before I met David – died of a drug overdose in Paris. Again, it seemed unreal to me; at that moment I had three young children and my world of suburban domesticity could not have contrasted more with his realm of shady deals and seedy street life. I felt infinite sadness that his life had been lived in the shadows, but I hadn't seen him for at least five years and it was an ambiguous pain.

My mother lived with us for more than twenty-five years. She didn't create the new independent life that I hoped for her after my father's death; instead she became a positive force in our young family and she was an outrageously delightful grandmother and lively companion for me when David was away working. She had maintained her journalistic whisky-and-cigarette habits, although she was rarely sick and didn't spend even one day in hospital from the time she joined us until the day she died. David always described my mum as a 'triumph of genes over abuse' and even though I was in shock when a sudden aneurism downed her in a matter of hours, I didn't feel her life had been cut short. I knew I would miss her dreadfully, but I felt her life had been fascinating and was worth celebrating. We took charge of the burial arrangements, bringing her back to the house the night before her 'home funeral' and having a festive party around the coffin in the middle of the kitchen table. Friends and neighbours gathered and we decorated the casket by communally painting it, writing messages and daubing footprints of the family pets (including the chickens). It was a riotous and joyful expression of love.

The following morning, I opened the lid of the coffin and looked at my dead mother. I immediately understood that she was no longer there; just a collection of cells; all that remained. I was washed by a sense that it was okay. Okay to die. Death didn't feel frightening or daunting. It felt normal.

My grief was expressed in an inability to clear out my mother's room and so for more than a year it sat exactly as it had been left on the day she died. The same sheets on the bed, the same pile of books on the bedside table and the same half-filled-with-urine commode that we didn't discover until eventually we decided the time had come to strip the space for another occupant. Mum was fastidious about emptying and washing her night potty so must have been feeling truly frightful on that last day, to have left it behind for someone else to deal with.

As I lie on the reclining chair next to Margaret in the middle of the night, I still don't know how I really feel about death. It's an unavoidable fact of life, it's natural, it's normal and all of us have to do it in the end. Even so it feels strange and mysterious, imponderable and abstract.

With routine morphine Margaret is now calm and seemingly pain-free, sleeping for long periods but also conscious at various times and able to cope with some thickened fluids. She's not interested in food. Fedema and I take it in turns to sit with her, playing the music she loves and allowing the sun to stream in through the large picture window that overlooks the garden. The palliative team come and go. They are reassured now that there's a settled care routine.

Ken shows me some documentation from their safe. It's a body donation agreement between Margaret and the medical school at the University of British Columbia in Vancouver. I'm not sure I want to think about all this right now, but he's keen for me to read and understand what's expected so that I can make it happen. He's no longer capable of handling complexities. Later I'll be grateful for this head start.

In the house there's an atmosphere of hushed anticipation. All the rituals of daily life continue at an unhurried pace – washing clothes and bedding, preparing meals and keeping the house clean and cheerful. There's a sense of time standing still. We drink a lot of tea and talk quietly about nothing much, certainly nothing important. It's as if we are observing ourselves and our surroundings in slow motion. The objective is that Margaret remains serene. I sit by her bed and talk softly to her, whispered words to let her know that someone is nearby. I hold her hand.

Watching Margaret's decline over the nine years of her dementia has confirmed my strong belief that the essence of her is still there, trapped inside her body and under the control of her damaged brain. The confounding thing about Alzheimer's is that every so often the sufferer will have a startlingly lucid moment. A smile, a turn of the head, eye contact. I cannot accept that there's 'nothing going on' or the possibility that all cognitive function has ceased. I refuse to talk about her in front of her, as if she's not there. I still love and respect her as much as ever: the clever, funny and kind woman with a sharp intellect and endless artistic talent. I can't see her as an empty shell. A nothing, waiting to die.

We have two peaceful days like this. Ken has accepted that Margaret is staying in her bed, and he pops in to see her often. He also talks to her, now with tenderness, and when he needs an afternoon nap we leave them alone together.

On the third night I fall asleep in the recliner chair beside Margaret as soon as I get comfortable. Keeping vigil is exhausting. I only stir when Ken gets up to go to the bathroom and I turn on the night light to check Margaret. I haven't been aware of her fidgeting or getting restless or needing pain relief.

She looks the same but isn't. Her hand feels warm but when I lean in close over her face I sense no breath. I feel for a pulse; there isn't one. She can't have been gone for long – perhaps only ten minutes. I check again, pulse and breathing. Nothing.

Ken comes out, heading back to his bed. I softly call his name and tell him I think Margaret has died. He comes over and, without his glasses on, leans close to her face. He feels her forehead, touches her hand.

'The palliative team say we can call them to come over any time there's a change – day or night,' I remind Ken. 'What do you want us to do? It's entirely up to you.'

In silence he stares at Margaret for another minute or two.

'I think we should all go back to bed and get some more sleep,' he says, 'and see if she's still dead in the morning.'

He turns and goes back to his bed. I switch off the light and tiptoe across the hallway to find Fedema. She's awake and has heard us talking, wondering what's going on. I tell her. We go down to the kitchen and make ourselves tea and toast. We talk for four or five hours until Ken finally wakes.

We check on Margaret, and she's still dead.

The morning after Margaret's death is a Saturday and Canada's Memorial Day. I phone the palliative care team to inform them that Margaret died peacefully in the night. They'll organise a doctor to sign the death certificate and a funeral company to come and collect her body within two hours. I also let them know I'll be contacting the University of British Columbia in Vancouver to organise the body donation. I knew this was a really important decision for Margaret; she'd talked about it when we first got back together. I also know that she wants no formal funeral or memorial. She just wants to disappear.

I reread the paperwork, which dates back more than eighteen years. It requires legal authorisation from Ken as next of kin and also indicates there will be additional legal forms to fill in, sign and to get witnessed either by a notary public, a bank agent or a judge. If wonder if they will still accept the body once they know the cause of death was Alzheimer's.

The Monday will be a public holiday and I'm anxious about how I'm going to get through all this red tape with most businesses, offices and banks closed. I find an 'after hours' contact number for the authority at the university that deals with body donations. They must be well aware that people don't just die during office hours.

A very pleasant woman takes my call, explains that she will need to email me some up-to-date documentation to print out, get signed, witnessed and returned to her before Margaret's casket can legally be loaded onto the ferry for the journey to the mainland. Then she informs me that the body must be at the university no later than Monday night. They won't accept a cadaver more than three days after death. I have less than three days, including a Sunday and a public holiday, in which to print out the paperwork, get it signed and witnessed and returned to the university – plus organise the release of Margaret's body and get it transported it to the university via the ferry. I feel overwhelmed but determined to make this happen for my sister.

I have a laptop computer with me, but no printer. I will have to dash to the supermarket and get a USB stick to download the documents, and then find somewhere to print them. Over the weekend, where will I find an authorised person to witness the documents?

Just as I'm leaving the house, the phone rings. It's the funeral director. They are unable to get through the CBD of downtown Victoria because it was closed off for the annual Memorial Day Parade. They won't be able to get out to the farm until the late afternoon. The same predicament applies to the palliative care team and the doctor who needs to sign the death certificate. They ask if we can prepare and dress the body, as too much time will have elapsed by the time they eventually make it out to the farm.

I speak to Fedema. Neither of us has laid out a body before but she is more than willing to help me do it. We search through Margaret's wardrobe and find some lovely clothes – her best. I've never seen her wearing them.

Suddenly the logistics of getting Margaret's body to Vancouver seems immaterial. We close the bedroom door and fill two basins with warm water. We delicately remove her pyjamas and there she is naked and dead, as fragile and vulnerable as a baby bird fallen from the nest. We work together, on either side of the bed, weeping in unison. Keening. In one way it is a release, an acknowledgement that for her these last few years of adversity and suffering have finally come to an end. Knowing that this is the last time we'll touch her; tend to her. Fedema, who has nursed Margaret with such wisdom and kindness over five years, is deeply moved. Our tears mingle with the warm water as we sponge her down. We brush her soft silver hair, massage moisturiser on her face and hands, and renew the bed linen.

In death, Margaret's face is a mask. I carefully closed her eyes when I first realised she was gone, but her mouth is set open. Alzheimer's has stripped away any hint that her expression was once lively, animated.

When we emerge from the bedroom, the house is full of people. Ken's immediate family has arrived, along with his lawyer. People are making tea and coffee, handing around biscuits. Ken has solved the problem of the witness – he remembers the home phone number of his local bank manager, who is happy to come over and sign the paperwork. All I have to do is download and print it.

Ken then announces that he wants me to write an obituary for Margaret, to run in the newspaper the following Wednesday. Another deadline! I'll need to talk to our brother, Jon, in Australia, as he shared the same difficult childhood and can give me some additional background. I need to speak to her colleagues from the university; her friends in the art group and her oldest friend, who travelled with her from Australia in the 1960s. I certainly have my work cut out.

I don't sleep well even though I'm utterly exhausted and overwhelmed by the emotion of working side by side with Fedema to prepare Margaret for leaving her much-loved home. My brain is addled by the number of tasks I have to complete. All afternoon people have been streaming into the house; endless cups of tea and kindly conversations. Ken holds court and seems greatly buoyed by the warmth extended by friends, neighbours and family members.

Staring at the ceiling in the dark, my heart goes out to Fedema, who had recently lost her husband. In the Philippines her husband had been caring for their four young children for years with the help of her elderly mother. Fedema has always been in daily contact via the internet; skyping every morning when the children are doing their homework and having breakfast around their kitchen table. The timing worked well as it was the afternoon in Canada, when Margaret and Ken are used to have their daily rest.

During this time Fedema never indicated to me that her husband had health issues – I don't recall her ever saying he had to see a doctor. There had been no hint of a problem. I was at the farm two years ago when I received an urgent email from Fedema. Her husband had experienced sudden chest pain in the night – a heart attack – and had died before medical help was available. He was in his early fifties.

At the time I went immediately to Canada to take over; she flew to her village to deal with her shock and grief. She had left Margaret and Ken's farm before I arrived, and I had left to return to Australia by the time she got back. So we've never had a chance to really talk about what really happened or to discuss how her mother was now coping on her own. The next time I saw her was this very week.

There's something profoundly wrong with this situation, where a devoted wife and mother is 'in service' caring for an elderly person in a foreign land. Laying out the body of my dead sister yet unable to be at the bedside of her husband. Unable to physically care for her own children and her ageing mother.

I will never feel comfortable with it, and now that Margaret has gone, I wonder what Fedema's future will be here. I'm quite certain Ken will want to keep her on, possibly as his own primary carer. But how long will it take for her children to be legally able to join her? The original employer contract stated two years, and Fedema has met the five-year requirement of the department of immigration for a 'family reunion'. I wonder, too, if Fedema does succeed in getting them to Canada, whether they will ever feel at home in this strange and very different culture. Will they have been permanently scarred by the years of separation and by their father's sudden death?

I wish I had a magic wand!

On Monday, miraculously we manage to get Margaret's body to the last ferry of the day, with just twenty-five minutes to spare. I even manage to write and send off the obituary.

Unlike in Australia, where a newspaper obituary is usually written by a member of staff, in the local *Times Colonist* anyone can have an obituary printed – at a price, of course. The larger the obit the more it will cost, so I decide to keep Margaret's life story short and sweet. In any event I'm quite certain she would have hated anything long-winded or obsequious.

And although I know Margaret was absolutely opposed to a funeral, I see no reason why we shouldn't have a gathering of friends and family at the farm. I can't tolerate the idea that she can just die and disappear without a trace. She loved a good party, and I'm determined to give her one, even though Ken is a bit dubious. He doesn't think many people will show up, as Margaret has been retired for nearly twenty-five years. He's wrong.

A few days before I am booked to leave for Australia we organise a high tea with cake and scones, champagne and canapés. The farm's packed to the rafters with friends and family, work colleagues and neighbours. I realise this gathering is probably more for my benefit than for Margaret, allowing me to celebrate the life of my sister with the people who knew and loved her. It's a necessary part of my letting go; acknowledging that I will no longer be needed to sit at Margaret's side.

I haven't been back to Vancouver Island since Margaret died. I kept in touch with Fedema, who stayed to care for Ken until he too died some two years later. It took Fedema nine years in total to wade through the red tape and bring her four lovely children from her home town to Canada. By this stage they were in their teens and the adjustment period was lengthy and at times very difficult. Now, I am pleased to report, they all seem very happy (and grown up). I have very fond memories of those years staying with Margaret, Ken and Fedema even during the difficult stages of Margaret's disease. I loved Margaret's friends and Ken's extended family and I hope one day to return and catch up with everyone.

23

A hopeful time

THE FARM, DECEMBER 2012

At Bathurst airport David is waiting outside, at the fence, the wind from the plane blowing his beard sidewise. I can't believe his beard has grown so much since the end of chemo and that he appears so well, so healthy and just like his old self. It's easy for me – and for him, too – to slide into the fantasy that the cancer has completely vanished. David hasn't searched out any negative information about his condition; instead he's been reading about 'miracle' survivors. People who've been told they are terminally ill, yet have emerged after five years cancer-free. These are the stories he chooses to read. This is the outcome he's hoping for.

David equates acceptance with giving up. Surrendering. Fighting is his nature; it's in his Celtic DNA. During the entire radiation and chemotherapy period, he spent endless hours delving deeply into his family ancestry via one of the popular genealogy websites. Being David, of course, he managed to sidestep all the 'extra charges' they invite you to pay to access the maximum information. Instead he has done the hard yards himself, meticulously putting the pieces together and peeling away the centuries to follow his family tree back to the fourteenth century. There are many aristocratic figures in the family's past and this tickles David tremendously. It seems appropriate that during a time of his life when it's difficult to look forward, looking back is bringing excitement and contentment. It's his way of rounding out his life, of making sense of who he is and his place in the scheme of things.

His external appearance of having been 'miraculously' restored to good health further convinces us that everything is going to be okay. It's amazing how easily we can fool ourselves into believing the treatments have worked.

Christmas is looming, and I've traditionally hosted our family celebrations. Twenty-five at the Leura house, and then fifteen at the farm at Yetholme. However, after the twelve months we've endured with David's diagnosis and treatment and then the death of Margaret, I'm contemplating doing something completely different. Something more self-indulgent that doesn't require getting up at 5am on Christmas morning to light the wood stove and stuff a turkey. I can recognise that I'm suffering from a degree of emotional and physical exhaustion.

Sunday morning in bed, reading the weekend newspapers, I notice a last-minute sale of berths on a liner doing a Christmas cruise around New Zealand. The itinerary is tempting to David, whose first job was in the merchant navy, servicing several ports that will be visited on this trip. He has a sister and her family in Wellington, where the ship will dock on Christmas Eve. Nostalgia, family and relaxation. It's a perfect solution and we book our places on the ship that will leave Sydney Harbour several days before Christmas.

I've never been interested in cruising. As a walker and a traveller who likes to push the boundaries – to step a little outside my comfort zone – the notion of being trapped on a vessel with 1000 other people doesn't really appeal. I grew up at the beach and I love the ocean, but my heart is in remote, difficult-to-access and wild places. Mountains and valleys. Villages and traditional ways of life. On the upside, I won't be peeling four kilos of potatoes on Christmas morning and I might even recapture the art of sleeping in. When I wake at dawn, as I have done since I had my first child, I'm drawn into the garden. There are always ten jobs to be done, and this is the best time of day to do them. I can easily get lost out there, for hours and hours. On a cruise ship there'll be no garden enticing me from my warm bed. Maybe this will be the first 'proper' holiday I've ever had. After decades of constantly travelling with groups, this will be my time to relax and do nothing. In forty-three years David and I have seldom holidayed alone – maybe twice. It's my turn to surrender.

What a different packing experience – a swimsuit, a few floaty frocks and some evening clothes and high heels. No trekking boots or backpack. No emergency first-aid kit or high-power headlamp for those inevitable trips to the toilet tent at 2am. Lots of books to read and my camera.

These last twelve months have been the most concentrated time I have spent with David in all our decades together. Our careers have kept us both on the move, mostly in opposite directions. All those years living in Leura, while David had his production office in Sydney, we only ever caught up at the weekends. Him filming overseas, sometimes for five or six months at a time. Dashing off to the Cannes Film Festival. My Himalayan adventures and my escape to France for six months. Now we're spending all our time together and I feel incredibly at ease with our relationship. We have been through so much together – fabulous times and frightful times. This suddenly feels like the right time; the precious space we have been waiting for all these years. Most of the pressures that kept us walking a financial and career tightrope for years and years have lifted. There's a sense of freedom from responsibility. I am sixty-two and David is seventy-three, so this enforced 'retirement' has come sooner than we expected. Yet we've embraced it. Bring on the holiday!

On Christmas Eve we dock in Wellington Harbour and are met by David's sister, Gillian, and her extended family. What a delight! She hasn't seen him since his diagnosis and it must be reassuring for her to see him looking so well and happy. We're glowing from our days at sea, new friendships we've formed and the fun of exploring the South Island.

There's a family lunch, which is a true celebration. A long overdue catch-up between three generations of his much-loved family. David is in top form and it's hard to imagine that he has been so sick this year.

We have Christmas day in Auckland, where David lived in his twenties. We walk around despite a bit of rain and it's fun to check out his old stomping ground. We've booked into a swish restaurant for a traditional lunch and it's the first time since childhood that I haven't been a kitchen slave. We wander happily back to the ship which leaves the port at 5pm. We have a snooze and skip dinner – all very civilised.

The rest of the cruise is relaxing, although I'm beginning to feel like – and resemble – a stuffed turkey. Too much food and not enough exercise, even with our two brisk deck walks every day. We love the Bay of Islands, which David knows well and we enjoy two days at sea on the way home. We know that we'll keep in regular contact with our new friends from Maine, the ship's chaplain and his wife. David, in particular, has benefited from his free-ranging conversations with the chaplain, voicing his concerns about life and death. Mortality. Maybe he found it easier to share his feelings and his fears with a stranger; someone with a philosophical and spiritual view of life. Someone who was not directly involved with or affected by his illness. I'm just delighted to see him engaged and happy.

24

Family times

THE FARM, JANUARY 2013

David and I feel really happy about our holiday, our batteries recharged for the year ahead. Even though I don't admit it to myself, or to David, I sense that these shared good times are really important for us. I don't take anything for granted any more.

Despite escaping our Christmas duties, January will make up for it because this is when we have as many of our grandchildren as possible to the farm for an extended summer holiday. Our place is the ideal setting for this: twenty-five acres partly landscaped, partly natural bush. A creek, several dams and some friendly companion animals – dogs, cats, chickens, ducks, geese, alpacas, sheep and goats. There are new lambs and kids, which the children always love cuddling and playing with. As well as the native animals, birds and reptiles that share our acres – kangaroos, wallaroos, swamp wallabies, wombats, echidnas, tortoises, blue tongue lizards, copperhead snakes, kookaburras, wild ducks and cockatoos, both black and white. Many more birds than this, of course, and the usual skinks, spiders, mice and rats – both introduced and native. The old farmhouse is huge, with lots of bedrooms, and the community hall out the back is great for rainy days.

In early January I do the seven-hour drive from the farm to the remote township of Hay, the meeting point where I pick up Miriam's four lovely sons, ranging in age from twelve to nineteen.

They live in Adelaide now, so we have an agreed arrangement of pick-ups and drop-offs because Hay is geographically the half way point between us. It also gives me a chance to have a catch up with Miriam, who I miss so much since the family moved so far away. We generally take a few rooms in a local motel and go out to dinner at the local club. It's a talkfest – we're a garrulous family and this next generation seems to have inherited the jocular gene. Lots of laughter and teasing and sharing of stories. I love the good-natured humour of my family.

Early the following day Miriam drives back to Adelaide and the children and I head back to the farm to enjoy an easy dinner before the 'real work' of the holiday begins. In the morning our son Aaron's ex arrives from Mudgee with her teenage son and daughter. Aaron also lives in Mudgee and has remarried. My ten-year-old grandson from the Blue

Mountains joins us with his family and we start as we mean to continue – with a huge, long sit-down family lunch. As we skipped Christmas the grandkids have requested roast turkey with all the trimmings. Even the crackers and presents! It's quite obvious I didn't really dodge my Christmas early start, lighting the wood stove at 5.30am (in the January heat) and stuffing the turkey. Kilos and kilos of potatoes to peel and roast in duck fat. Beans and pumpkin from the garden, a pavlova with our own free-range eggs, raspberries and redcurrants. It's exhausting but delightful.

As three of our children are into their second marriages, we now have a very modern blended and extended family. We wanted to maintain relationships with our three 'outlaws' – after all, they're the parents of six of our grandchildren. This hasn't always been easy, but we've grown so fond of them that it just doesn't seem feasible to lose that connection because of divorce. The farm is neutral territory and it all seems to work in a very commonsense, civilised way. This January we have an extra teenager staying – my remarried ex-son-in-law's stepson, who goes to school with a couple of his step-siblings. He was sad when he knew they would be disappearing for three weeks so we invited him to join us.

The grandkids help David clear the table but he won't let anyone help with rinsing and stacking of the dishwasher. He's transferred some of his OCD tendency into this clearing-up ritual, which means that I'm absolutely off duty from the moment the meal arrives at the table. Everything – from teaspoon to roasting pan – is meticulously washed and returned to its rightful place in the pantry. He continued with this clean-up routine right through his really rough period with chemo and all its side effects. It's a matter of pride. It certainly makes having the grandchildren to stay for three weeks a much easier task – they are given plenty of other jobs to do, of course, both inside and out. One is tasked with making two loaves of bread a day; one with watering the vegetable garden. I get them picking fruit, mucking out animal sheds and even painting. One summer they repainted all the shed doors and did a great job. The older ones are taught how to use the tractor and do some mowing and slashing for me. Many hands make light work.

My rule is no television, mobile phones, iPads or computers when the sun is shining. Parents seem to have a lot of trouble enforcing rules like this but somehow the kids take it from their grandparents. In any event the novelty of being at the farm, which they all love, and having their cousins to hang out with, makes it okay. When it rains they're given some leeway – a movie perhaps or a computer game. I also encourage them to play board games and card games and the younger ones always resort to Lego if they're trapped indoors by the weather. Town is twenty-five minutes away and we drive in to see new-release films – either in shifts or both David and I take our own vehicles, four kids each. We also take them to the local swimming pool and a massive adventure playground that they love because of the flying fox. It's a busy time, but I can't imagine anything that I enjoy more. I never feel more like myself, more real, than when I have my grandchildren around. It's a feeling of being complete, but it's also the fact that I feel so well-loved in this setting. A big old comfortable house surrounded by glorious gardens and paddocks, places to walk and have picnics where the children can climb trees and splash in the stream. I love cooking, especially big meals for the family, and the kids really appreciate being able to take it in turns to choose their favourite meals. You offer love and you're given so much love in return – why wouldn't I feel complete?

The younger grandchildren visit us with their parents at various times during the three weeks – for Sunday lunches and so we can take the annual 'grandkids' photograph as the family builds. I treasure these records of our expanding and growing family. Babies turning into toddlers, then into preschoolers and kindergarten kids in uniforms. Before you know it, primary and then high school. It all happens in a flash, and this photo ritual and their progressive height measurements pencilled on the kitchen door frame help me to keep a handle on it. I would love to have the little kids as well, but their hands-on care would take away from the time and energy that I can spend on the bigger kids. Their turn will come.

Towards the end of the holiday, on a day that's too hot to play around the paddocks, I take the kids into the adventure playground for a picnic with the promise of afternoon at the pool. After packing the picnic remnants into the car, I decide to have a turn on the flying fox that keeps the children entertained for hours. Climbing into the harness, the kids give me an almighty push, but before I've adjusted myself properly.

Somehow my thumb gets caught in the mechanism and I feel a surge of intense pain as my thumb is virtually wrenched from my right hand. Trying not to faint from the agony, I get myself untangled and sit on the ground, deep breathing. I follow up on my promise, and take them to the swimming pool, cradling my hand and watching as a vivid blue stripe develops across my hand and up my arm. I fear I've done some real damage.

Eventually I drag the kids from the pool over to the hospital casualty department. Negotiating a four-wheel drive ute with one hand is tricky, but somehow I manage. We have to wait a while, then the X-ray shows nothing broken or dislocated. They suggest I return the following day for an ultrasound, which will detect any ligament or tendon damage. I drive the kids back to the farm but quickly realise I am virtually incapacitated, so it's all hands to the pump preparing dinner – kids peeling potatoes, making gravy, setting the table. The following day my ex-son-in-law from Adelaide arrives to pick up the boys. He's staying for two nights before doing the long return drive, so I manage to slip into the hospital for further investigation. Sure enough, the main tendon of the thumb has been badly torn, and I'm sent across to the fracture clinic to see the orthopaedic surgeon. The clinic is just one big room where we all sit nursing our wounds and waiting in turn to be seen by the specialist. This style of clinic means we can all hear every word between patient and doctor, and it's not lost on me that all these injuries are the result of our stupid behaviour. There's a woman, maybe two decades younger than me, with a fractured leg from falling off her children's backyard trampoline; there's a man who removed the safety shut-off option on his ride on mower, who was run down and injured when he got off to remove an obstacle on the lawn; there's a prisoner from the local gaol, who's handcuffed to a policeman. He got into a fight with a fellow prisoner and had his arm and collarbone broken. So when I, in my sixties, have to confess to the surgeon that my injury was caused by riding on a flying fox in the local children's adventure play-ground, I feel more than a little ridiculous.

'You seem to be making a good living from people behaving like absolute idiots,' I comment, and he laughs.

He tells me my hand will require surgery – quite a complex operation. The sooner the better. He books me in for the following Monday, when the kids will have all gone home to their respective families. It's rather a dismal way to end the holiday, but I know that despite the pain I'm feeling right now, I will be desperately sad to see them all go.

That night we have a big farewell dinner, prepared mostly by the kids with David clearing up. The coming year is a great unknown for us. He seems so exuberant and he's also loved having all the grandkids to stay. I feel as though we're entering an unknown stage: watch and wait. A sort of limbo, standing by to see if the cancer will return.

25

A new family member

The farm seems very quiet once all the kids have gone, especially as we are without a dog to keep us company. We've always had dogs. Even before we owned our first home I managed to sneak an adorable border collie puppy into David's small bedsit – absolutely against the real estate rules. We called him Wombat and he lived to be eighteen years old, a treasured member of the family, especially when the kids were growing up. Since that time we have owned a springer spaniel and two golden labradors. During the time when David was sick we had another old labrador called Jasper – we inherited him from Aaron when he moved to a rental that didn't allow pets. Jasper had been a bit of a wild dog in his youth, but age had finally slowed him down and he was a wonderful companion who was absolutely trustworthy with the children and loved coming with us on long rambling walks, even when his back legs started going. It's a common problem with ageing dogs of this breed and more than once I was forced to wade waist-deep into the dam to push him out when he got stuck. We would try, without much success, to keep him from plunging into the water the moment he saw it but eventually we have to change the route of our walks, giving the dam and the creek a wide berth to stop Jasper from getting bogged and unable to free himself.

Six months ago Jasper died of old age and for the first time we've been without a dog in our lives. While David's in remission I decide to remedy the situation and phone a pug rescue organisation to see if they have any dogs that need a new home. David had loved a pet pug his family owned when he was a child, and I thought having a pug around might be a comfort or a distraction. They do have a dog available – a black female about eighteen months old. Her name is Bonnie.

Rescue dogs are not free dogs. There are considerable costs to pay – mostly for the vet check they perform when a dog is rescued or surrendered, and also for the care and maintenance of the animal until it's adopted. There are many volunteers involved, however the whole process of caring for these discarded and mistreated animals is costly.

They didn't tell us why Bonnie had ended up in care but hinted that her previous owners lived in an upstairs flat and that both worked long hours which meant that the animal had been left alone for most of the day and often well into the night. It had made her neurotic and clingy.

A friend from Melbourne is staying with us when the phone call comes to set up a rendezvous with the rescue people and take ownership of Bonnie.

The three of us drive to Richmond where they are waiting for us – the dog is so pretty with her glossy black coat and bright shining eyes. She seems very nervous so I sit in the back holding her on my lap, reassuring her all the way home. We keep her on the lead and walk her around the garden, then take her inside, where she seems to settle down quite quickly. She's introduced to Sid the cat without too much drama, and I really hope she'll fit in with our family life.

Bonnie's not an easy dog, certainly compared to the three labradors we owned over the years. She doesn't like being left alone, which we understand, and she stays as close to us as she can. I don't want a dog sleeping in our bedroom, and we manage to train her to sleep next to the fireplace in her own little bed. She accepts this without much fuss, especially as David is inclined to stay up late. He takes her for a long walk outside before settling her down for the night. Then from the moment he gets up in the morning she's firmly glued to his side. He takes her out for a pee – she doesn't like to be outside on her own so it means wandering around with her waiting for her to do her morning business. Then all day she's at his feet under the desk, or trotting behind him everywhere he goes, even to the loo.

This separation anxiety makes her a demanding compan-ion. You can't just open the back door and let her outside for a run; you have to go with her, in all weathers. When she's inside with us she's not content to just curl up at our feet. She wants to be on the sofa, or on our laps or better still up behind us on the back of the sofa. This puts her in the 'top dog' position in the family, a status she feels is rightly hers.

She loves coming on our long walks and takes off after the small gang of kangaroos if she spies them at the back of the farm. They are irritated by her and I don't blame them. She's hard work but at this stage we have the time to indulge her demands. And David adores her.

The grandkids also love Bonnie and they dote on her during their lengthy visits. She loves having the kids around and even leaves David's side to take up with them. She's never really attached to me – unless there's nobody else around. She's affectionate, funny and very entertaining and I'm pleased I made the decision to adopt her as she and David are inseparable.

David is looking and feeling healthy enough for me to consider going ahead with another yoga trek in India. He's very keen for me to continue my working life as if nothing has changed and I can't quite decide if it's part of his cancer denial, or a panic about my needing to continue to earn an income for us. For me, the anxiety about leaving him on his own for several weeks is very real, however his last round of tests have been very positive, with no sign of the original tumour in his oesophagus.

My hand is healing well after the surgery and I've been gradually regaining strength by getting back out into the garden and by doing yoga at least twice a week. Both these activities are like magic to me. Yoga calms me, slows me down and helps me to let go of a lot of internalised stress. Apart from the physical benefits of stretching, the simple act of stopping everything and lying still on a mat seems to bring me serenity. While I'm absorbed by the flowing movements and postures my mind is only on the yoga practice and not on the worries of my life. Yoga gets my blood flowing and releases feel-good endorphins as well as stilling my mind. It's the same in the garden. As I move around the vegetable beds, weeding, watering and harvesting for our lunch, I'm absorbed and distracted. There are real, positive benefits from touching the soil. I dig into and turn the compost, syphon liquid fertiliser from the worm farm and dilute it with water. This potion transforms the soil with goodness, and the plants are smiling at me. I feed kitchen scraps to the chickens and gather their eggs to make a custard. Sometimes I wander out for ten minutes after breakfast, and I'm still pottering around three hours later.

My other 'go to' remedy for stress is drinking wine but this only has short-term benefits and ultimately it adds to my anxiety. It has a blanking-out effect but also makes my sleeping patterns erratic. I try to limit the wine to a convivial glass, or two. I don't always succeed.

While I'm planning my trek and keeping up with the garden, David has been busy with his ongoing family ancestry research and oral history recordings of his work in the Australian film industry, which he's been doing by phone with a colleague from Melbourne. He's also been communicating with many people from his life – old friends from his New Zealand days; extended family members and people he's loved working with over the decades. I see these pursuits as a healthy and satisfying way to fill his days. It's all reflective stuff – looking back rather than forward. Reconnecting with people who have been important or influential in his life. Talking to them, explaining his medical situation without being negative or melodramatic.

The upshot is that we have a steady stream of visitors to the farm – from all corners of Australia, indeed the world. David has not said 'I am dying' but he has said his future is uncertain and that if people want to visit us, it should be sooner rather than later while he is robust and energetic enough to enjoy special time with people.

I think it's marvellous, and almost every week we have lunches or overnight visits from a wide range of friends and associates. The friends from overseas stay longer – up to a week at a time – and David is delighted to show them around the property, our local hamlet and our nearby country town. Naturally it's a lot of work, but it's a form of therapy and his mood is greatly elevated when we have people with us at the farm. So many shared memories, pored over, laughed about and re-examined.

After people leave and the house is quiet, we are left alone to pick over the conversations and the memories. This is hugely beneficial for both of us. The process of discussing and analysing events and memories from David's life somehow helps us to clarify and make some sense of it all. Patterns emerge; themes are repeated. It's not that we reach any resolutions or conclusions, it's just that we gain insight and perspective from hindsight. At times these post-mortems can be painful – especially when we touch on that period when our marriage was rocky. Yet it feels positive to lay some of the demons to rest.

We don't talk about tomorrow, only yesterday.

26

A short-lived escape

INDIA, APRIL 2013

Our sons organise a good load of firewood to keep David going while I head off to meet my yoga trekking group in India. He's looking quite strong and has no trouble wheeling barrowloads of split logs to the back door to transfer into the family room with the efficient wood heater. As usual he drops me at the local airport, and I don't feel anxious about leaving him for just two weeks. I never tire of India. Kolkata is over-whelming in size and population yet it's the energy of the people that I find uplifting. There's a buzz and a vitality that shakes me up, reminds me I am alive. The light is different from Australia. Possibly it's the haze that lies over the metrop-olis contrasting against the vivid colours of the women's clothing. Everything seems heightened and more intense. The group I'm leading is all female – women of a certain age who like to walk, to do yoga under the guidance of their teacher from Bathurst and experience a shared adventure.

We fly to the outpost of Bodagra and drive to beautiful Darjeeling in the hills. We spend a few days sightseeing, visiting tea plantations and monasteries before driving by bus to Yuksom and starting our trek to Dzongri. It's spring in the Himalayas, a perfect time for walking.

We make camp and do yoga practice in the late afternoon before dinner in the mess tent. Everyone's tired from the long drive and we hit our tents early, sleeping well because of the altitude. Before breakfast and after morning tea, we again throw down our mats and do some yoga stretches, which will set us up for the long, steep walk.

The terrain is varied and so is the flora. We walk through mixed forests of oak, birch and maple with flowering chest-nuts, magnolias and rhododendrons. There are silver fir trees and a diverse understorey that includes orchids, poppies, primulas, gentians and even wild gladiolus. Our walking is sometimes convivial and chatty, sometimes silent and medi-tative. We naturally fall into several small groups walking at different paces. In the early mornings it's misty when we set off, and the pace is slow but steady. Most days we walk for at least six hours; some days a bit more. There's a lot of uphill walking at first, gradually levelling out as we head towards the highest point at 4020 metres.

Spectacular snow-covered mountains surround us. The peak of Kangchenjunga is 8586 metres, and we also see the mountain range that separates Sikkim from Nepal, the Singali Ridge, which has numerous peaks over 7000 metres.

The days are warm, the nights are cool to cold. Our tents and sleeping bags are cosy and we're given down-lined jackets for sitting around in the evenings. The food, prepared by our little team of cooks, is delicious and much appreciated at the end of a long day's walking. We're given a lesson in making chapatis – hand-rolled dough that is fried and delectable. We all crowd into the small cooking tent and the young cooks are obviously delighted to share their skills with us.

Every day we're given a hot lunch along the walking track. It never ceases to delight me when we turn a corner and there are blankets spread out on the grass or over rocks, and rows of bright tiffin boxes filled with hot rice and vegetable curries, flatbreads and freshly sliced salad followed by fruit and hot tea. We feel very spoilt by our crew.

Our gear is carried by dzo – a cross between yaks and domestic cattle. They are tremendously strong but also comparatively placid, having inherited good genes from both parents.

When we finally get back to Darjeeling at the end of the trek I phone David from a funny little booth where the operator squashes inside with me – dialling the number and taking my money at the end. David is absolutely fine, has been cooking for himself. He does admit he's looking forward to my return. Even though he says he's feeling terrific, I sense he's become dependent on my constant monitoring of his health and wellbeing. I'm more than comfortable with that. I want nothing more than to be at his side.

27

A true celebration

It's winter in Yetholme and we put on a fantastic birthday lunch for David on a crisp late June day. Our daughter Miriam comes from Adelaide, as well as all three of our boys and their wives and partners plus six of the grandchildren. David's ex-wife and her partner come up from Sydney for the occasion, plus one of my son's ex-wives and her new partner. It's an inclusive, no-holds-barred, extended-family party. It's the first time in years we have all our adult children together and they revert to their childhood behaviours of teasing and general skylarking.

The farm is terrific for occasions like this, there's plenty of room for everyone. The old farmhouse has weathered the years extremely well. I don't like overly fussy or decorated rooms – possibly a backlash from the years I spent working as a journalist on a popular interiors magazine. As long as my home is warm and comfortable, I'm happy. I've never rushed out to buy new furniture and we still use the feather-stuffed sofas my parents bought in Sydney after the war. There are rugs I've collected on my travels and a long dining room table which we had built while still in Leura. It can easily seat fourteen and a few more at a pinch. The kitchen is a bit country style but not that different from how it would always have been. I've not changed much about the place, just added a modern stainless-steel gas stove and a timber chopping block. I still use my mother's copper-bottomed pots and pans, and the cast iron skillet that she brought back from America in the 1940s. Having a no-stress house like this is terrific when there are a lot of children around – I'm never anxious about kids making themselves at home.

I haven't seen David so happy and relaxed in a long time. He cuddles babies; debates with teenagers; drinks champagne and does all the table clearing and dishwashing unassisted. David dislikes sharing the clean-up and will allow no one else to stack the dishwasher.

Miriam and I have a few quiet words about how every-thing's going along. She wants me to be truthful about his progress and the ongoing attitude of the medicos. However, at the party nobody really touches on the subject of illness or death except to tease him a bit about his hair loss, in that affectionate way that families do.

I'm not celebrating David's birthday because I think it will be his last. If Dr Death is accurate about the twelve-month average survival rate, David won't be around to see seventy-four, but I won't allow myself to think like that; I'm just taking every opportunity to celebrate his life.

Who among us really wants to talk about death? It's the forbidden subject. The taboo. If the person who's dying wants to talk, then it opens the door for a conversation. David just doesn't want to talk about it. He might make a few jokes about Dr Death or the terrified social worker, but a general family discussion around the possibility of dying is not in his repertoire.

Most of the family stay overnight and we all have break-fast together before they head back to their various homes – in Sydney, the Blue Mountains and Adelaide. Again, it's just the two of us, in our safe farm bubble.

28

Not what I was expecting

It's been nearly a year since David finished chemotherapy followed by a scan that revealed the primary tumour was no longer in evidence. We knew there were still rogue cells in there, but he's been looking and feeling in excellent health. He's had two more routine follow-up scans and after the second one we were booked in for a meeting with our new oncologist.

I was feeling confident and expecting the new specialist to say everything was still just fine. There was no trace of bad news on his face or in his body language when he welcomed us into his rooms. From my perspective this was nothing more than a routine visit.

Not so. He holds up the scans and points to David's liver. We can see numerous shadows there, both large and small.

No mistaking it, the cancer is back. David is calmer than I have ever seen him. He even smiles and tells the doctor that he sensed something was not quite right.

I, on the other hand, am in a state of shock; rendered speechless. How could David have sensed this and yet said nothing? He kept saying he feels terrific. He looks terrific with no external clues to warn me. If indeed he believed the cancer was back, why didn't he warn me? I'm poleaxed. Many months later this same doctor will tell me he'd never seen anyone look as shocked and dismayed in his life. There's no way I can disguise my feeling of devastation. It's a bombshell.

Immediately we make a booking to start a second series of chemotherapy treatments, starting in just ten days' time. The thought of David having to endure another six or eight infusions of toxic chemicals fills me with horror. Another five or six months of suffering ahead. Back to square one. I can barely speak in the car on the way home to the farm. In contrast, David seems resigned and philosophical about his situation. When we arrive home he wants to make love, saying that once the chemo restarts there can be no more nookie. I couldn't even imagine becoming aroused the way I'm feeling – I'm looking forward to a glass of wine to numb my pain instead. Yet I know intimacy is probably what David needs at this moment, my arms around him and my love. I find it very difficult not to cry.

Later I phone the children and David also calls the closest members of his family – his brother and sister. They both live overseas and he's very keen for them to come and see him.

The sooner the better, as we know that the chemo has accumulative side effects. After two or three rounds he may well not feel like seeing anyone at all.

A visit is immediately organised, but it can't be until after the second session of therapy. I make especially delicious meals during that week leading up to the first infusion, knowing that very soon he won't be able to eat: everything will be tasting metallic and unpalatable. I'm very frightened.

The marvellous oncology nurses welcome us back like old friends. David is given his usual room with a view and I stay at his side for the whole five hours. I've brought in some soup and bread from home. We chat, he snoozes for a while, then it's time to go home. He manages to eat a small dinner but already some side effects have started kicking in.

By morning he's feeling absolutely terrible. In my diary I write, 'David is down. Pain? Discomfort?' The following day I write, 'Call oncologist at cancer clinic very bad reaction to chemo.'

We're given some stronger anti-nausea drugs and the specialist decides to slightly amend the chemical cocktail for his next session. They had started on the 'last line of defence' with very strong drugs. He's obviously unable to tolerate them.

Gradually the side effects settle down and again we start receiving visitors. More than ever, since David's now telling people that the prognosis is not good. I have a couple of work gigs booked that I can't cancel. One is a garden talk for the committee of the Leura Garden Festival. It's bad timing because some old friends – our former GP and his wife – are coming to visit that day. They now live in Tasmania and it's the only chance they will have to see us. I leave food for David to heat up and kick myself that I will miss seeing them.

I also have a group of students booked for a workshop in Goulburn. I sometimes do 'memoir-writing workshops' and more than a dozen would-be-authors have enrolled for a full day. I can't cancel and it means staying overnight as the workshop starts early. I'm very anxious about leaving David on his own when he's feeling so hideous. He manages very well, although when I return he's developed a new and uncomfortable complication; his hands and legs are very swollen and painful. Again I phone the oncologist in a slight panic.

David's younger brother and sister, Charles and Gillian, come for four nights and it's absolutely wonderful to see them. By now David is looking pretty shabby. His hair and beard have rapidly vanished, his skin is blotchy and flaky and he's started dropping weight dramatically. In spite of this he manages to lift his energy levels to make the most of this special family reunion. The three of them walk to every corner of the farm and talk about their childhoods and their parents. They laugh and catch up on their latest news. It's nearly a decade since all three of them have been together at the same time so it's an intense but essential get together. I stand back a little, giving them space. We're all really sad when this precious together time comes to an end.

Christmas is coming and the chemotherapy will continue until after the New Year. It's difficult for me to get excited, or to shop for presents for our grandchildren. I buy gifts for the little ones and give the older ones money. I just don't have much creative or mental energy to spare.

We never speak of death or dying. We just take each day as it comes and live in the moment.

Very little is written in my diary about this period. Page after page is empty. I can only summon up the memories by looking at the photographs from that Christmas: the grand-children arriving; the shared meals; picnics by the dam; the annual family photograph – this time with a lovely new grandson Jake, baby brother to Alena. Now we have eleven descendants – eight boys and three girls. That photo of us with them all, under the big cypress tree at the front of the farm, haunts me. David looks happy but most of his hair and beard have now disappeared. His face has a shiny, ruddy appearance – the effects of the chemo. The three tallest grandsons are at the back, one holding Bonnie the pug, and our oldest granddaughter holding the new baby boy. It will be the last snapshot of us all together.

Before the cancer returned, I'd confidently put together an itinerary to take another yoga group to the Himalayas – this time to the Annapurna ranges in Nepal. I was lulled into a false sense of hope: that David would continue in his false 'remission' indefinitely. However, when I suggest to him that the trip should now probably be cancelled or delayed, he becomes agitated and insists that I proceed as if nothing is wrong. This determination of his, that I carry on regardless, is a bit disconcerting. Not wanting to cause him any further stress, I allow the travel company to continue taking bookings for the tour even though I fear it will never happen.

Some of our dearest and oldest friends came to see us during this time – mostly for lunch. David isn't eating much because of the ongoing side effects of the chemo, but he always rallies when our guests arrive and is at his most charming and ebullient. Memories stir and his words flow. There is nonstop laughter. I know the significance of these get-togethers. David holds his friends and work colleagues in very high regard, and he's making sure to spend time with as many as can get out to the farm. His special way of saying thank you, and goodbye.

In between times, he sleeps a lot. His energy levels are very low: he'll lie on the bed intending to read and almost immediately fall asleep. We try to see a film at least once a week, but he no longer has the energy to go for long rambling walks. During the day I relax my 'no dogs in the bedroom' rule and Bonnie's bed is put on the floor next to David. She's a good sleeper too.

The drugs are affecting every part of David's body. The skin on his hands and feet becomes red, dry and split. He's advised to stop washing so frequently and to stop using soap. It's a bit confronting for a man known as a compulsive hand-washer, but he agrees and starts rubbing his poor hands with rich moisturising creams instead. His body hair has just about vanished. His gums feel terrible; his teeth seem to be getting wobbly and his eyesight has deteriorated.

He doesn't complain about any of this. He mentions symptoms, of course, and asks our GP for advice on dealing with side effects. But he's remarkably accepting – even sanguine – about the entire process. For me, watching from the sidelines, it's gruelling. I hate to see this breakdown of his naturally healthy body and wonder if it's all worth it. I've heard of cancer patients being killed by the chemo, and I feel this is happening before my eyes. I don't want David to see how anxious I'm feeling. I try and muster a little of his acceptance.

The weeks turn into months, with one day of chemo every three weeks. By March 2014, the chemo has come to an end and David is immediately sent for a scan of his liver to see if there has been any improvement. He has another meeting scheduled with the oncologist the following Wednesday. One way or the other, we will know where he stands.

I've never felt such dread at the thought of a meeting. David looks so terrible, so drained and exhausted. I can only imagine the news will be bad.

The night before the appointment with the oncologist we sleep poorly. I feel coiled up, like a spring. David is jumpy and seems breathless in his slumber. We drift in and out of sleep in fits and starts then face the day looking wrung out.

The doctor greets us warmly and immediately puts the scan up on a light box to clearly show us what's going on inside David's war-torn body. Crunch time.

'Quite good news actually,' he says. 'The chemo has been effective once again, and even though there are still some tumours in evidence, everything has retreated considerably.'

Huge relief sweeps over me. He suggests a maintenance plan to keep David stable with a low-dose chemo tablet that, hopefully, will stop the tumours from aggressively growing back. The doctor is so encouraging.

'We can keep you going for quite a time with this type of treatment – maybe nine months, maybe even a year.' I cling to those words. Nine months. A year.

David is examined, mostly to check out the side effects on his skin. I can't really remember at what point I mention the breathlessness I observed during the previous night. I know I brought the subject up, but somehow this piece of information is lost in all the other back and forth about ongoing treatment and the possibility of reducing the side effects.

His last words to us are that he'll organise the prescription for the low-dose medication, but suggests David has the rest of the week free from treatment – a bit of time away from the chemicals – and starts the new regime the following Monday.

As we float out I keep replaying 'nine months, a year; nine months, a year' over and over in my head. We are clutching at the lifeline of hope that has been thrown to us. More time, more precious time.

David shakes the oncologist's hand, thanking him for all his care and expertise. It will be the last time they ever see each other. Ten days after the euphoria we experience at this consultation, David is dead. He doesn't even get a chance to start the 'maintenance regime' of chemo tablets because from that day onwards everything goes pear-shaped.

29

The tipping point

After celebrating the possibility of yet another reprieve with champagne (mostly me) and a special dinner, we collapse into bed early, exhausted by the emotional stress of it all. Less than two hours later David wakes me in distress. His breathing has suddenly become laboured: he's gasping for each breath. He wants to go to the hospital; he needs help.

I drive in the dark straight to casualty. It's not busy and they are quickly able to settle him down with breathing support. He's unable to speak for long, so I give the medical team his full history and describe our visit to the oncologist only this morning.

Once he's fallen asleep I drive back to the farm, tossing and turning for a few hours before returning at 7am to see if they've worked out what's wrong. A chest X-ray reveals an enlarged silhouette of his heart, with what appears to be excess fluid in the pericardial sac. This is confirmed by a CT scan showing the fluid that's constricting his heart, causing the breathlessness. This condition is called pericardial effusion.

We see the registrar, who explains that it's not an unusual side effect of cancer treatment. We've never heard of it; no mention has ever been made about side effects to the heart. And yet later in the day when I google it, end stage cancer is listed as one of the major causes of fluid around the heart. I guess they can't warn you about every possible nasty side effect – the impact of chemotherapy on the whole body is profound.

In my shock I don't ask any of the right questions: 'How is this problem treated? Can it be resolved?' Most certainly I didn't ask, 'Will pericardial effusion kill him?'

In spite of the serious diagnosis David wants to go home. He's desperate to get out of hospital and even though the registrar is hesitant, they allow us to leave. His breathing doesn't seem to be as laboured as last night. Maybe it's settling down; resolving itself.

Of course, what the professionals are seeing is a man with cancer who now has a serious complication. He is therefore dying and quite naturally wants to be at home. What I am seeing is a man with a temporary setback. Nobody said to me, 'He cannot survive this'.

That night around the same time David wakes again in a panic and struggling to breathe. Again, we drive into casualty and he's admitted quickly and given oxygen. It's a frightening scenario. He settles to sleep; I drive back to the farm.

When I wake, very early, my brain goes into overdrive because I suddenly realise I'm supposed to be getting on a plane to Nepal in just eleven days. Everything has been booked and paid for – flights, hotels, local guides. I'm sure half the trekkers have already started packing their bags for this adventure. I can't see myself going anywhere anytime soon.

I take food from home into the hospital for David's lunch. He isn't eating much, but he has an aversion to the hospital menu and would eat nothing if I didn't bring in something he enjoys. I remind him about the upcoming Nepal trip, saying I intend to cancel it. He vehemently disagrees. I don't appreciate it at the time, but David has ongoing anxiety about our financial situation and even though I only earn a modest fee for organising the treks, he's insistent that I proceed. I had planned to have a haircut before flying out, so I quickly organise an appointment, fearing that if I continue debating the issue with David, the agitation might worsen his condition. As it is, he's so short of breath that talking at all is a huge strain.

I don't have the time it takes for a full appointment with colour and streaks. I asked the hairdresser for a super quick cut and colour. What colour?

'Oh, why not make it bright red,' I suggest. 'I'll just be the mad old hippie chick in Kathmandu.' She takes me at my word and I emerge with red hair so vivid I look like Lucille Ball on acid. David yelps in horror when he sees me and even the doctors look nonplussed at my sudden change in appearance. I hope the colour will calm down after a few good washes, and laugh it off.

I stay with David into the evening, quietly reading while he sleeps. Eventually I drive back to the farm, to another restless night of worry. When I return the following morning his condition has deteriorated considerably and the next two days are harrowing. There's no cardiac specialist who can operate in Bathurst, and we've been told the fluid around his heart needs to be drained away to make him more comfortable. He can have no relief from breathlessness until this happens. There are two very supportive young doctors, and they've been phoning various big city hospitals to get him transferred for urgent surgery. After a morning of calls, it appears they can't get him into any of the major public hospitals in Sydney.

'Why not?' I asked naively.

The response flattens me. 'It's difficult to book surgery for end-stage cancer patients,' I was told.

End stage? He's dying, is that what's happening? Nobody's mentioned the 'D' word, and I'm struggling to interpret medical euphemisms. I could ask the direct question, but I don't. Instead, I opt for being proactive.

I make two calls. Firstly, I call our old friend John, a cardiologist from the Blue Mountains. He's the most dedicated of men, both as a physician and as a friend. For the last year he's been conducting a pacemaker clinic in Bathurst Hospital every month and knowing of David's condition he regularly called in for a cup of coffee and a chat. It was a great comfort to us both.

Surely John will know what to do next. I leave a message.

Next I call World Expeditions to tell them the news. There's no way I can go with the group, they'll just have to go without me. I was sorry, really sorry, but we're in a critical situation and I must remain at David's side. They understand without question. They reassure me they can sort something out; I must not worry.

John calls me back within twenty minutes. He's found a top cardiologist – a good friend and colleague – who will accept David as his patient. He works at one of Sydney's biggest private hospitals. David can be transferred by ambulance almost immediately and the surgery would be the following day. I'm shaking with relief.

Smiling, I dash back to the ward to tell David and the young doctors the excellent news. We have a surgeon and we have a hospital. We can leave as soon as possible.

David explodes. Despite his breathless state he's shouting and gesticulating like a crazy man. 'I'm not going to a private hospital! No way. Absolutely not. It will cost thousands and thousands of dollars. I'm not going!'

The young doctors look as shocked as I feel. I suggest they leave now while I sort out this 'little hiccup' in proceedings. I tell them to go ahead and book the transfer ambulance.

By now, David is almost hysterical and I try my best to calm him down. He has to see reason.

We've had private medical insurance for more than forty

years but have really only used it for the extras – teeth, eyes, physio. Once we did use it when I had a lower back injury that ended in painful spasms. I was transferred by ambulance to a private hospital and the 'gap' payment was outrageously high. David has never forgotten or forgiven this experience, and has assiduously avoided private hospitals and fee charging specialists ever since. Talking him around isn't going to be easy.

All the patients on the ward are staring at us. I draw the curtains around the bed and sit as close to him as possible. I take his hand.

'Why the hell have we been paying for private medical insurance for all these years?' I hiss into his ear.

'I don't care. I'm not using it. It will cost thousands and thousands. I won't go.'

Unlike me, he isn't whispering.

'We've been paying insurance premiums just for a moment like this. It's an emergency, don't you understand? Without taking this fluid from around your heart, you will die!' Now I'm sobbing.

'I'd rather die than pay the gap,' is his irrational response.

I lose it.

'I don't care what you want, you are getting into an ambulance and we are going to Sydney. You will have surgery tomorrow. John has organised it. You trust John, don't you?'

'Of course I trust John. I just don't trust those other bastards.' His last words.

By now he's gasping for breath.

'We are going, and that's that.'

I leave him and go to the doctors' station. They have called an ambulance transfer. I return to the ward, pack his stuff into a small bag and kiss him stiffly on the forehead.

'I'll see you at the hospital,' I say as I leave.

He's no longer speaking to me, his face like thunder. I make my getaway before he changes his mind and starts shouting again.

I can't believe what's just happened. David at death's door and in need of urgent intervention, yet we've been having a screaming argument about what it might cost. I can't believe how insane it all is. The very last thing I want is to distress him or for him to be angry with me. How do normal people cope with these situations?

30

The moment of truth

THE HOSPITAL, MARCH 2014

At the farm I pack enough clothes for myself for two or three days. I phone our children and update them on the situation. I phone the hospital in Sydney, tell them we're on the way and ask what accommodation is available nearby. Tony and his lovely family live in Sydney but they're at least forty minutes from the hospital. I don't want to be dealing with peak hour traffic getting back and forth to see David – I want to be as close as possible.

There's a motel a five-minute walk from the hospital and I book a room for two nights. David will never know this – I tell him I'm staying with the family. I don't wish to compound his anxiety about expenditure.

I arrive at the hospital in Sydney just as the ambulance from Bathurst is pulling into the reception bay. I greet David;

he is thin lipped and terse. While they take him up to his private room, I fill in the admission forms and hand over our private insurance card. I am asked to pay a deposit – around $120 dollars – and they reassure me that the rest of the expenditure will be covered by our insurance.

In his room, someone's brought him tea and a sandwich. We speak quietly and I tell him about the conversation with the cashier at reception. He doesn't believe it, of course, but he certainly seems calmer now. Perhaps he's been given something to settle him down – I don't ask. We sit together for an hour, I hold his hand and we talk about the following day. I can see that he feels a certain relief – at least now something will happen to counteract his chest pain and breathlessness.

When I leave the hospital to go to my motel I feel greatly consoled, and pleased that I'm staying so close by.

I've no inkling that this will be the last rational conversation I will ever have with David.

Although it's late, I update the children, then I crash into bed and an exhausted sleep, totally drained by the distressing events of the last few days. Very early the next morning, walking down to the hospital, my mobile phone rings. It's a nurse: David's highly agitated and keeps asking for me. I pick up speed to get to his bedside as quickly as possible.

I'm not prepared for what I find. The cardiac specialist – John's colleague – has come in early to prep David for the surgery. However, David's pacing the floor, waving his arms in the air and shouting at people. I've seen him when he's angry; I've seen him being unreasonable and even irrational. This is quite different. He acknowledges me brusquely and demands to know where in the hell I've been. Why I wasn't with him during the night? He's rambling and talking nonsense. Every so often he turns to the surgeon and hurls some abuse. Attempts to placate him are useless.

'You don't know anything. You're a fucking moron!' he shouts at the specialist.

I'm confused and horrified. There's no justification for this behaviour and to me the scenario is surreal, as though I'm caught in the middle of a deeply disturbing nightmare.

I'm also acutely aware of my appearance, with my outrageous scarlet hair. What seemed like a bit of fun at the time has left me feeling at a disadvantage. This medical team has never met us before – David's acting like a raving lunatic and I look like I've overdosed on LSD. I realise it sounds trite, but I wonder if they will take anything I say seriously. I've never had to deal with such a critical situation before, and I really wish I look more like my real self; my more plausible self.

One of the nurses manages to distract David so I can have a few quiet words to the doctor in the corridor.

'He wasn't like this last night,' I sob. 'He was absolutely fine, very calm and reasonable.'

'Something has happened to him during the night, so we need to run a few tests before he can have the surgery,' he tells me. 'We need to make sure he hasn't had a stroke or that any other neurological episode has caused this behaviour.'

Strangely I remember very little about the following few hours. I must have been in severe shock. It felt as though I was simply observing something that was happening to someone else. I sit with David, he calms down when everyone leaves the room and he even sleeps a little. They must have given him something to pacify him. He appears disoriented when they wheel him away for the brain scans. At least he isn't ranting and raving.

While he's being tested I start making urgent calls. First to the children, then to David's sister and brother, both overseas. Finally, I accept that this isn't going to end well. It's time to convey this message to those who need to know.

I talk to Miriam in Adelaide.

'Do you want me to come, Mum?' she asks. She has a very demanding fulltime job and four boisterous sons. I know taking time off will be tricky for her to organise.

'It's up to you. I totally understand how difficult it is.'

I am trying not to cry or to convey my own distress.

The doctor finds me in David's room, staring blankly at the wall. The scans show that David hasn't had a stroke, so he's being taken straight down for the surgery. He should be in recovery and then intensive care within the next three hours.

Optimistically I convince myself that the surgery might be a game-changer. That once the stress is taken from his heart, his mental state will return to normal. He will be weak, he will need my full support, but he will return to being the David I know and love. Not the disorientated, rambling madman I witnessed this morning.

The next time I see him is in the intensive care unit. He's hooked up to various monitors with a drainage tube coming from the side of his chest. At the end of the tube is a bag that's slowly collecting the fluid draining from his heart. He's subdued and for the first time in days his breathing is easy. I sit with him as he drifts in and out of the anaesthetic. He looks at me and half smiles. I squeeze his hand, reassuring him that it's been a successful operation. I don't tell him that the cardiologist drained almost two litres of fluid from around his heart. The pericardial sac is meant to contain about half a teaspoon of fluid as a protective cushion for this vital organ, and various doctors comment that David must be as strong as an ox to have survived such a massive weight compressing his heart.

As he regains consciousness, his agitation returns. His eyes dart around the room in alarm. He doesn't understand where he is, or why. When he speaks, it's a jumble of disconnected words. My hopes for a return to rationality are dashed. I feel so alone and helpless. There's nothing I can say or do that can change what's happened.

Our daughter calls to say she has managed time off work and is booked on a flight from Adelaide early the following morning. A huge wave of relief washes over me. My Sydney daughter-in-law, Leslie, new baby in arms, arrives at the hospital and sits nursing the infant in the foyer ready to give me some respite whenever I need it. She repeats this vigil on my behalf every day that David remains in intensive care. She knows I can't do this alone and is just there to support me. Every few hours I go down and sit with the sleeping infant, and have a sandwich and a cup of tea, while she stays with David in intensive care.

David is mostly sleeping and when he does awake he's befuddled and extremely grumpy. Our son Ethan comes down from the mountains and stays for several hours. David responds positively to the visit – he even manages a smile. His language is still jumbled. He leaves words out of sentences and gets very frustrated if we can't make sense of what he's trying to say. Later I learn that during this whole post-operative period David is quite heavily sedated to keep him as calm as possible.

One of the intensive care specialists gives me some insight into David's delirium. He believes it was caused by severe dehydration in the days before he came down to Westmead Hospital. The medical team in Bathurst had reduced his fluid intake in an attempt to slow down the build-up of fluid around his heart – it all makes sense. Sadly, it had the effect of tipping his metabolism to the point where he could no longer think clearly.

I phone a couple of my closest friends and they come to visit us at the hospital over the next few days. Although unable to speak, David obviously recognises them and seems quite alert, if silent, as we sit chatting. They speak to him, of course, but his responses are confused and it actually makes him anxious to try and communicate. Ironically, it's the opposite of how he's always been. Over the years I've some-times become irritated when my old friends come to visit us at the farm because David has always tended to monopolise people to the point where I find it hard to get a word in edgewise. Now he can't speak with any clarity and I wonder how it must feel for him, being trapped inside a brain that's no longer able conduct a meaningful conversation. In some ways it's reminiscent of my sister Margaret as she slipped further and further into Alzheimer's. Losing the power of her voice.

I keep hoping, quietly to myself, that any moment the old David will reappear. That whatever chemical or metabolic changes that caused his confusion will suddenly reverse. Hope is a powerful state of mind. I've always been a positive person and hope manifests itself deeply in my psyche. I live in hope that somehow everything will be okay. Not allowing myself to imagine that it won't.

Throughout this entire illness I've tried to avoid thinking about David's death, although occasionally I've pictured the end of his life as being a slow but intimate time. I've imagined myself sitting at his bedside, holding his hand and saying all those important things about our love and the joy of the decades we have spent together. Now I sense there will never be another logical conversation. All those things will remain unspoken. I can tell him I love him, and I do, but he can't say all the things he needs to say.

I could never, ever, have imagined it would end like this.

I realise that the yoga trekking group must be flying out from Sydney to Nepal around now. It's difficult to comprehend that the rest of the world is carrying on in a normal everyday way while I'm immersed in this intense life and death struggle.

My daughter-in-law Lynne comes down to the hospital with some of our grandchildren. Only small groups of visitors are allowed into intensive care, and everyone takes it in turns to spend time with him. When Miriam arrives and everyone gathers around, I feel stronger and more able to cope.

I now accept that David is dying and we discuss, as a family, the need to get him back to the farm. He hates being in hospital, and I hate the prospect of him dying in this clinical environment. I've developed a good rapport with the intensive care registrar and I propose to him the idea of taking David home.

From their perspective, the issue is the drain from his heart. There is always a risk of infection and he tells me that usually patients aren't allowed home with a heart drain in place. If they remove the drain the fluid will start building up again and we'll be back to square one.

The surgeon visits and we discuss all the pros and cons. I ask him if there's anything else that can be done for David if he remains in hospital. There isn't.

He points out that David's Advanced Care Directive was quite specific about not wanting intervention at the end of life. When he was first diagnosed we decided to update our wills, appointing various children in key roles such as power of attorney, enduring guardian and making me executor. David wrote a legally binding directive about his end-of-life medical treatment, in which he asked for there to be as little intervention as possible in the natural process of dying. I was asked to bring this when we booked into hospital, and picked it up when I was briefly back at the farm on my way through. The surgeon said that even draining the fluid from his heart could be deemed as excessive intervention. However, he pointed out that from a palliative care perspective it could be totally justified as it made David much more comfortable and no longer struggling to breathe, which was so stressful and exhausting. As stressful for those watching the struggle as for David himself.

The two doctors deliberate and decide that David can indeed go home, as long as I have plenty of support from the extended family and the palliative care team where we live. I point out that our daughter has a degree in obstetric nursing and is highly skilled at managing pain relief. I also tell them that Ethan and Lynne have a disabled daughter, Isabella, who has been tube-fed to the stomach for more than a decade. They are more than capable of managing the tubes for draining fluid from the heart. It is agreed.

With joy I tell everyone, including David, that we can go home. He smiles, he actually smiles, but can't seem to grasp why we must wait until an ambulance is available for the transfer. He wants to go home to the farm, and he wants to go right then and there.

In the afternoon there's a terrible drama. David wakes from sleep in a complete panic. It takes me a minute to realise the reason for his distress – he needs to go to the toilet. I try to restrain him, he's started climbing over the railings of the bed, and I repeatedly press the buzzer for help. The nurse closes the curtain and brings him a bedpan which he knocks roughly out of her hand. He's shouting, screaming abuse and pulling at his monitor cords and at the heart-draining tube. Full panic ensues, a loud alarm sounds and staff are running from all directions. Two burly wardsmen pin him down and a doctor injects some sort of rapid-acting sedative into his bum. He continues to swear, shout and struggle then suddenly stops, panting for breath. In spite of the sedation he is just as determined not to use the pan.

I'm sobbing at this point, and begging them to just let David do as he wishes and take him to the toilet. They disconnect everything except the drain, lift him into a wheel-chair and take him to the loo. When he returns to the bed he's calm but exhausted. He sleeps for hours and hours.

When he finally wakes he's again agitated. He can't find the words, but it's quite obvious he wants to go home. He waves his arms around, pointing at the door and remonstrat-ing with anyone who passes. I try to explain we just have to wait, but it's now getting late and I fear there will be no ambulance until the following day.

When he does his evening rounds, I apologise to our kind intensive care doctor for David's outrageous behaviour. He smiles and puts his hand on my arm.

'Quite frankly, we prefer patients like your husband because they still have such fight in them. They may be angry and difficult to manage, but we can see determination in their eyes.

'The patients who just lie still with fear in their eyes, they're the ones we find the most challenging. Seeing that fear and not being able to take it away is much harder for us to cope with.'

His words immediately reassure me. I'm not surprised, really, that David is battling for his dignity to the very end. He's always been a fastidious man and there's no way he will yield to being forced to change the habits of a lifetime. No bedpan for David! I applaud him.

It's now Saturday morning, nearly twenty-four hours since the patient-transfer ambulance was called, and I wonder how much longer we'll be waiting for one to become available. David's like a raging bull, gesticulating in the direction of the door and grunting. We have another repeat of the toilet episode, with staff running from all directions as David manages to climb over the metal railing and barge headlong in the direction of the bathroom, unassisted, tubes and cords stretched to the limit. This time they get him into a wheel-chair and do what he wants. They realise there's no point fighting him. One of the nurses tries to comfort Ethan by pointing out that his father really can't be blamed for his behaviour, because of the delirium.

My son smiles. 'This is absolutely the way I would expect my father to behave in this situation.' We manage a laugh.

Back at the farm, Lynne has descended with a car full of food and other supplies. She strips all the beds and remakes them with clean sheets; does loads of washing and starts cooking soup and pasta sauces for a large number of people. There are five fireplaces in the farmhouse and she lights three of them to warm the place up. Yetholme is at altitude – around 1200 metres – and can be one the coldest places in New South Wales. The fires don't just make the place cosy, they offer their own familiar comfort. She picks flowers from the garden and fills vases for every room. The house will be warm and welcoming if and when we finally arrive.

After lunch I'm feeling very anxious, worried that David may well die before we can get him home. Our daughter and I sit with him as he drifts in and out of sleep. Every time he wakes he motions to the door, questioning. We try to reassure him.

I dash down to the toilet on the ground floor and on my way back I see two ambos wheeling a trolley across the foyer towards the lifts.

'Are you here for David Hannay? I ask.

'Yes,' they say.

I can't hold back my tears. I go back up with them to intensive care, and the look on David's face when he realises what's happening is beyond joyful. Yet again he has to be restrained – from trying to leap from the hospital bed onto the trolley without waiting for any assistance. I really don't know where he gets these sudden outbursts of incredible strength from. He's unstoppable; his human spirit cannot be thwarted.

Our daughter Miriam decides to drive our car so I can

ride with David in the ambulance. The medic sitting in the back with me tells me that unfortunately they can only transfer us as far as Katoomba Hospital, where we'll have to wait for a second ambulance from that region to become available for the last section of the journey out to the farm. He's sorry about this, but it's a busy weekend and they will be needed back in Sydney for Saturday evening.

I don't really care, as long as we are on the way. David is determined to stay awake and he keeps sitting up and looking out the big windows to see how far we have travelled. He keeps pointing and saying 'Where?' We give him regular updates. Homebush Bay. Penrith. Blaxland. Springwood. He needs routine pain medication along the way and it sends him straight to sleep. Before we reach Katoomba the medic has a quiet conversation with the driver, then gets on his mobile phone to ambulance headquarters.

'I believe it will be in the best interest of the patient if we don't leave him at Katoomba and therefore we're taking him all the way to Yetholme.'

He isn't asking permission, he's informing them of his decision.

'Can you actually do that?' I asked, tears streaming down my face.

'Indeed I can,' he says, smiling broadly. 'Once we're on the road it's our call. No decision can be made at headquarters. It's up to us to decide what is best for the patient.'

I have never felt such intense gratitude in my life. We are going home. *Home.*

David continues to sleep, unaware that he'll be at the farm in just over an hour. When we turn into the bumpy driveway he sits bolt upright and looks around. I can't see his face because I'm strapped into a seat behind him, but I can tell from our medic's expression that something lovely is happening. David knows exactly where he is and is reacting accordingly. I touch his shoulder. The driver reverses the large vehicle as near as possible to the kitchen veranda, then goes around to swing open the doors. At that very moment Ethan and Lynne emerge from the house, smiling and rushing towards the ambulance. David throws open his arms and, although I still can't see his face, his delight is mirrored by theirs. We are home.

31

Home

Home. We give the ambulance men a quick cup of tea after they settle David into our big bed. I thank them profusely and almost immediately David drops into an exhausted sleep of relief. Everyone will be coming to the farm. Our ex-daughter-in-law Lorna from Melbourne, and two more of the grandchildren; Tony and his wife Leslie and their two little ones from Sydney; middle son Aaron and his wife Rachel from Mudgee and eventually Miriam's husband Mark and four sons from Adelaide.

Within an hour we've hit a problem we didn't anticipate. From the intensive care ward I left messages for the regional palliative care team to notify them of David's transfer, but now that we're here I pick up a message on the landline saying they close down over the weekend. We have the small quantity of morphine that we've brought with us from the hospital but not nearly enough pain relief to get us through the next two days and nights.

I contact our local GP, who agrees to organise some additional pain meds. He's a lovely man, very caring, but obviously a bit reticent to give us as much morphine as would be supplied under supervision by the palliative care team. It's a big responsibility, allowing people to administer possibly lethal drugs to close family members. We understand his caution, but Miriam's really concerned that we won't have sufficient morphine to keep him comfortable until Monday. Our GP came out and can clearly see that we are very well organised but sticks to a prescription quantity, which is well below what David was being given in hospital.

A roster is drawn up, so that one of the adults will be at David's side twenty-four hours a day. I will be with him too, in our bed during the night, but I will be trying to sleep because the children are determined that I get some rest and that I won't have any concerns about the logistics of their father's care. They work together as a tight-knit team. I can't even begin to express how loved and supported I feel and I know that David feels the same. Even though he cannot communicate coherently, his entire demeanour has changed since getting home. He's serene at last. No longer wild-eyed, agitated or belligerent, he's able to make his immediate needs – in particular the toileting but also the pain relief – easily understood. He's never alone, not for one second, and I spend most of the day propped up beside him, being brought cups of tea and then later glasses of wine and delicious food.

Someone is cooking, someone is entertaining the children, someone is splitting logs for the fire and someone is dashing into town to fill the prescriptions and get more food supplies.

Miriam gathers together every possible additional pain medication in the house, because she realises they will need to keep topping David up constantly. His mouth is incredibly dry as he no longer seems capable of swallowing even fluids, so administering the oral meds is a nightmare. They must be ground into a paste and put into his mouth in small increments with squirts of water so that they can be absorbed. The kids don't fill me in on all these troublesome details, as they don't want me to stress.

I manage to sleep that first night, at least six hours, with the help of wine and some calmative drug from the kit. I do wake several times, to see one or other of our sons slumped in the wingback chair next to David, dozing but still able to sense if he should move or become distressed. I'm deeply touched by this devotion.

I feel surprisingly refreshed in the morning and the house is buzzing with activity – children, animals, glowing fires and pots of tea. We have all gathered because David is dying, but I can clearly see that the situation is about as good as it can be given the circumstances. I can also see that Miriam is exhausted and I sense the burden of responsibility on her shoulders. However, she's also being well supported by her brothers and their wives.

I have a break, taking some of the younger children on a long walk around the farm. Winter is coming, the trees are turning and the colours are dramatic. I take comfort from the change of seasons and the presence of these precious young people in my life.

Later that day, our cardiologist friend John and his wife Di arrive. I hadn't phoned him but he has followed our movements by communicating with his colleagues at the hospital and knows we're home. His presence has such a reassuring and calming effect on all of us. He gives us some useful advice on ways to manage David when he needs to be moved in and out of bed, and David obviously recognises John, although he is unable to acknowledge him.

We manage to get some extra morphine, but John can see that we'll be struggling to keep David comfortable overnight. It's too late in the day to rectify this, because the weekend duty pharmacy has already closed. We can, of course, take him into the Bathurst Hospital but that's the very last thing we want. The situation will have to be desperate to subject him to another hospital admission.

In essence, the problem we're facing is the lack of regional palliative care over the weekend. It's crazy when you think about it – people can't choose a convenient time to die, and this support mechanism needs to be in place twenty-four hours a day, seven days a week. We have the expertise and the willingness of our family members to support David beautifully during these last days of his life but we don't have sufficient quantities of painkillers to keep him truly comfortable. He sleeps well enough, but is fidgety when awake because the pain keeps breaking through. He's certainly not writhing in agony, but he could be more tranquil.

The day passes and again I sleep at David's side, aware of the constant vigil through the night. Monday morning dawns and I wander into the garden to breathe the crisp, cold air. The palliative team is due to arrive before 9 am – we've been promised the first call-out of the day. They are to bring drugs and equipment, expertise and support. We eat breakfast followed by a flurry of tidying and organising. The relief when the vehicle arrives with two trained palliative care nurses is palpable. Miriam is shaking and tearful – the weight of the world has been lifted from her shoulders. Her response is understandable. Having trained as a midwife, she's kept meticulous notes of everything that's been done for her father. Every medication has been listed, with the dosage and time administered. Notes on his sleep, his toileting, his anxiety and restlessness. The team are impressed with how the family have managed and immediately organise medications for the next twenty-four hours. Through the port in his leg they give him an appropriate dose of morphine, the first proper dose in forty-eight hours. The change is rapid. At last, he's at ease. He sighs into the pillow and we all sigh with him.

It's a much more relaxed day, knowing that David's pain is finally being managed. It's the birthday of one of the grandchildren and a celebratory dinner is planned, with cake and some champagne for the adults. I spend most of my time fully dressed propped up on the bed with David, giving him a cuddle and chatting to whoever is 'on duty' for his care. I daydream that it could go on like this forever. David sleeping peacefully, me snugly beside him with all our family around. I worry a little because all of them have taken time off work to support us. How long will this last? I wish it could last forever.

Mid-afternoon I'm talking to Miriam, going over the events of the last few days. We're very careful not to speak a single word about death or dying, knowing that even when in a coma a dying person can be acutely aware of every word spoken around them. It's a relaxed chat – nothing intense – then suddenly David sits upright in the bed, wide-eyed and looking from Miriam to me. He speaks his first articulate sentence in almost seven days.

'Do I *look* dead?' he asks.

We're stunned but I respond immediately, placing my hand over his.

'You certainly do *not* look dead,' I say. 'Far from it.'

Slowly he drops back onto his pillow and closes his eyes peacefully. Satisfied.

Around dinner time, the spicy smell of home-cooked curry fills the house. The long dining room table is set and there are candles to help set the mood for a birthday party. Miriam suggests that I go and join the family for the first sitting of the meal – and when I've finished she'll swap places with me. But barely two mouthfuls into the meal, I am aware of footsteps running down the hallway towards the kitchen. Wondering what's going on, I leave the table and find Miriam and Lynne in an intense huddle in the kitchen.

'What's up?' I ask.

'Dad's breathing has changed,' Miriam says.

Back in the bedroom I get as close to David on the bed as possible. We're joined by everyone, the half-served birthday meal left uneaten on the table.

His breathing is intermittent. A rattle of breath, in short bursts. We all know what this means and we surround him. Toddlers, teenagers, a babe in arms. We lean towards him, taking every single breath with him. Watching and listening until suddenly everything stops. No more breath.

The combined howl of shock and grief is overwhelming. I look steadily at David, who's perfectly still, but I'm also aware of the keening in the room. It goes on; they touch his face, his hands. They stroke him and cry.

Someone – I'm not sure who – whisks the small children away. They've never seen their parents like this before and common sense says it may be too much for them to comprehend. They return to the dining room table to finish their meal . . . thankfully the cat is not fond of curry.

I have no concept of time but eventually the crying slows and we just look around the room – at each other and at David. I'm brought a glass of wine. Drinks in hand, we make a toast. We're completely drained, exhausted and heart-broken. Eventually the curry is reheated and plates handed around. We stay together in the room for hours – eating, talking, drinking and even singing happy birthday to the poor child, who's utterly bushed.

My memories of that evening are blurred, of course. All I know is I wanted to stay in our bed, to sleep beside David and feel his presence, even in death. In any event, there are no more beds available in the house – every sofa and blow-up mattress is occupied. I cannot imagine being anywhere else but by his side. He died a few minutes after 8 pm but it was well past midnight by the time we turn out the lights. I recall a feeling of numbness. Nothingness. Somehow during the night, in my deep sleep, I forget.

PART 2

After David

32

The days after

In the morning we slowly start making plans for the funeral. It's a Tuesday and we all agree that the following Saturday will be best, allowing people time to travel and organise accommodation. There's really no more space in the house so we book rooms for travellers in a nearby motel.

Our grandsons arrive from Adelaide in time to see their grandfather lying peacefully in his own bed. It's important for me that they have a chance to say goodbye to him in a safe, familiar setting.

John drives over to the farm to write the death certificate. Again, I haven't asked him – he's kindly anticipated this need. I'd never thought about a death certificate as anything but a dry official document. John treats the writing of it as something special and he's determined to get it absolutely right, especially from my perspective. We talk though all the possible contributing factors causing David's death – the end-stage cancer, the pericardial effusion, the delirium as a sign of organ failure. By stepping me through this process I feel not only included, but somehow an integral part of everything that's happened. I could never have imagined the writing of a death certificate as therapeutic, but it is.

Late afternoon the undertakers arrive. My Mudgee son, Aaron, whose work as a horticulturist with the parks and gardens department included managing the local cemetery, has worked with these men and recommended them. They're kind and helpful but not overly deferential, which I find refreshing. I didn't want anything phony around this funeral and their role is to be minimal. We want to maintain as much involvement and control as a family as we can.

This is also the way we managed my mother's funeral. It's a philosophy emerging from a desire to hold the funeral process and the deceased loved one as close to our hearts as possible. Having been to funerals where the eulogy was delivered by a celebrant who didn't even know the person who'd died, we're determined to make this gathering for David as personal and as real to his memory as possible.

After I sign the necessary paperwork I gather the grandchildren and we walk across the laneway to our little Anglican village church and cemetery, where David will be buried. The undertakers are taking David's body back to Mudgee and I can't bear to see him leave the farm this last time. Instead we will choose the position of the double plot we've purchased. There are some historic headstones here dating back to 1873 when the settlement was first established, including the headstone of the formidable woman Mary Walshaw who built our farmhouse in the early 1920s.

Aaron has a gravedigger's certificate and has offered to excavate his father's grave. I love this idea and he comes with us to help choose the best position. He prefers the vacant plots on the edges of the slope below the church. Knowing David, I advocate for putting him in an awkward place that's higher up, near the church and on the same level as the significant historic graves.

'Think about it,' I put to my son. 'Would your dad want to be in the back stalls or up in the dress circle where he would assume he belongs?' We laugh. It will be logistically tricky to operate the digging machine in this confined space and some of the excavating will need to be finished by hand, but I know it's where David would want to rest.

Our son Ethan is a skilled carpenter and decides to build his father's casket using local timbers. I'm moved by his desire to be so personally involved. He sets up his equipment on an area of flat lawn near the kitchen door to mill the timbers and creates the most remarkable coffin. Everyone takes a role in the days leading up to the funeral. Initially we plan to conduct the service at the farmhouse —speaking from the long, wide front veranda with our guests standing on the lawn. However, the weather forecast is ominous and we decide instead to hire the local community hall next door to the cemetery.

I'm consulted on every aspect of the funeral but I'm not expected to actually do anything very much at all. The family puts it all together – the printing of the memorial cards, the catering for the wake, the decoration of the hall, the order of the service, the music and the filming of the whole shebang. Every detail is being taken care of, so I spend my time phoning and emailing people to spread the news and hanging out with the grandchildren. I also drive into Bathurst and choose some soft velvety red fabric to line the casket.

Someone mows all the lawns – usually my job – and I in turn help prepare the constant round of lunches and dinners that are required to keep the family-and-friends team well fed. During this hiatus, between David's death and his funeral, I don't feel any overwhelming grief or sadness. I'm still numb and there's so much going on around me, and so many marvellous people to hug and talk to, that the reality of it just hasn't set in.

33

Into that good night

It was wonderful to see everyone, so many of whom had travelled from interstate, gathering to be part of this ceremony for David. I was overwhelmed by the numbers who kept arriving, and the chairs in the community hall quickly filled with actors and writers, film crews and financiers; my brothers, my cousins, our neighbours and friends from the mountains and dozens of contemporaries of our children, who had spent so much time hanging out at our place when they were youngsters. Such a mixed representation of his life, and of our lives together.

It's a fantastic day. Miriam's the MC; David's oldest friend from his New Zealand days delivers the eulogy; friends speak or recite poems; our grandson Sam represents the next generation, giving a touching and at times humorous talk;

Ethan plays his guitar and sings. There's so much warmth and laughter, and many rich memories are stirred. Two of the actors have come dressed in their character's wardrobe from the bikie film, *Stone*, that David was involved in back in the early 1970s. To the soundtrack of that same film, David's heavy homemade casket is wheeled from the hall and up the road to the cemetery, everyone following in a long procession, holding hands and sharing more stories.

When my mother died, David was working on a film project with a prominent Indigenous actress who told him of their tradition of adopting a native animal or bird as their totem, their spirit. My mother loved currawongs, a bird with an aggressive reputation yet the most beautiful carolling song. As we lowered her casket into the ground the entire gathering evoked a chorus of currawongs calling – it was spine-tingling and I know she would have loved every moment of it.

David had chosen the majestic black cockatoos that live in the forests around our village as his totem. At certain times of the year they travel in great flocks, very high in the sky, and their cacophonous calls flood the air for days at a time. More commonly they travel in pairs or small family groups, swooping low and screeching along the way. They are huge creatures who crash clumsily into the tree branches when landing and create havoc below as they recklessly pluck, peck and discard pine and cypress cones. Frequently they hang upside down from the branches in a comical fashion, eating and calling to their friends. During the service I invite our guests to send David off with the call of the black cockatoo.

It's more a high-pitched shriek than a call, and I deliver a not-very-plausible rendition as an example.

At the graveside everyone gathers and the casket is slowly lowered into the ground with a black cockatoo chorus to see him on his way. One of the actors, true to character, lights up a joint, takes a deep drag then symbolically throws it down to David. There are half a dozen shovels so everyone has a chance to help cover the coffin as a final gesture. I'm still numb.

The party goes on for hours, with finger food, cake and cups of tea and champagne; followed later in the day by a huge barbecue with even more wine and beer. I tiptoe away quite early, exhausted, but am not surprised to hear the hangers-on still carousing at three in the morning. They're invisible when I get up the next morning. Some have camped in the community hall out the back and I also notice tents pitched in the paddock. We don't see them until later that day, looking a bit shabby. It certainly has been a raging send-off for my dear old bloke.

34

Reality hits

THE FARM, APRIL, MAY, JUNE 2014

Gradually over the following few days everyone leaves, returning home to pets and school and work. As each carload exits down the long farm driveway, I feel a sense of heaviness. They've all been fantastic and have worked so hard, with such love, to get me through this ordeal. Now it's over and life must return to normal. Whatever that means.

The last to leave are our daughter's husband and four sons. I give them David's car to drive back to Adelaide. I'll fly over at some later stage to pick it up. My plan is to sell it and keep the farm four-wheel drive ute for myself.

When Miriam decides to use compassionate leave and stay with me for two weeks, I'm overwhelmed with relief: I'm not quite ready to face the future alone. As the car turns onto the laneway, we stand together, staring at nothing. Eventually

I turn towards the kitchen door. All can say to her, my darling daughter, is: 'I could never, ever have imagined feeling so dreadful'.

It's true. I'm utterly drained and exhausted, and I feel a crushing sense of emptiness. It's as though a sword has sliced off a segment of me, of my body, leaving me limp and bleeding. Where to next?

My daughter and I do everything we can to cheer ourselves up – light the fire, make soup, drink wine. As the executor of David's will, I have a lot of business to attend to and I'm relieved she'll be here to help with it.

The simple fact is that I've never had anything to do with the business or the money side of our lives together. For forty-three years I had chosen to practise blissful ignorance about money and all its ramifications because David has managed the ups and downs of our fiscal circumstances. We never really had 'proper jobs'. As freelancers in creative industries, even for the ten years I worked on the *Gardening Australia* team for the ABC, I was a contracted freelancer rather than a fulltime employee. David's films and my books had always been one-off deals and our income varied dramatically from year to year. It takes skill to manage this moveable feast, and quite frankly I had very little interest at all. I was happy to work – I loved the diversity and creativity of my career. But I had never sent out an invoice or banked a cheque or paid a bill.

So now I was faced with learning the ropes, with no inclination or enthusiasm and certainly no previous experience.

Knowing that I would end up in this position, I wonder, why David didn't walk me through the basics to make the transition a little easier? I believe that for him to hand over this responsibility to me would have been the final admission of defeat. It would have been like saying 'You had better get your head around this because I am not going to be around to help you.' Knowing that I was reluctant didn't help either, and so we both just pushed the issue to one side.

We began our investigation into the finances by fetching the huge folders that contained years of bank statements, neatly filed in order. David had been meticulous in keeping our records in perfect order. (The desk itself was always a complete mess of paperwork, but invariably he knew what was where and could put his hand on whatever he needed.)

We stacked the folders on the kitchen table, and I poured a large glass of wine before delving into them. I was trying to work out what bills were being paid on a regular basis so I could continue without falling into arrears. David had refused to use internet banking and every week he would stand in line at the post office, cheque book in hand, to pay each bill as it fell due. He prided himself on paying on the last possible day each account needed to be settled, although sometimes he realised a bill was overdue a day or two afterwards and he would then phone the power company or internet provider in a panic with lengthy explanations and excuses. He rarely, if ever, was charged interest. I knew there were also a couple of bills he paid over the phone, and I suspected they were our credit card bills.

We needed to go into town, to our bank, and let them know that David had died. I had been issued with the official death certificate and was told that I would need to have certified copies made to give out when proof of death was legally required. Having this job to do, getting on top of the finances, was a good distraction from my grief. I was less inclined to curl up in a ball if I knew I had important deadlines to meet. I tried not to feel overwhelmed by the task ahead.

At the bank, I handed over David's death certificate and our accounts were immediately closed and our credit cards cancelled. I hadn't expected this, and was dismayed when I realised that now all I possessed was the cash in my wallet. The cheerful woman at the bank suggested I open a new account in my own name, which I did, but without any funds to go in it. Miriam offered to lend me some money to get started but I was mortified. How can we even do the shopping?

Then something amazing happened. When we arrived back at the farm, there was an envelope in the letterbox with a cheque for several thousand dollars in my name from the Department of Communications and the Arts. It is my annual royalty payment for copies of my books borrowed from libraries. The Australian Lending Rights Scheme legislation was introduced during the time of good old Gough Whitlam, to compensate authors (and publishers) for the loss of potential sales income due to their books being available for use for free in public libraries and educational institutions. The scheme pays a few cents every time a book is borrowed or photocopied for research. It adds up slowly over of twelve months.

So, for the first time since I was twenty I had my own bank account in my own name containing my own earnings. Crazy.

I have always been fiscally reckless. When I first met David, at 21, I had been working for five years but had not submitted an income tax return. I had slipped under the radar and it was a ridiculous situation because the tax had been deducted from my weekly pay slip but I had never claimed my rightful refund. David jumped into rescue mode, made contact with my ex-employers and gathered up copies of my group certif-icates. He did my overdue tax returns and eventually I was sent a healthy refund cheque. By this stage we were together in a relationship and had established a joint bank account.

Now, reluctantly in charge of my own finances, I started looking at our regular outgoings to estimate how much a month it would cost me to live. In a notebook I wrote down all the regular payments: medical insurance, car payments, utility bills, phone and internet. I kept coming across monthly deductions from insurance companies which made me feel a little excited. Maybe David had some life insurance policies that he neglected to mention to me? Perhaps there will be an unexpected windfall? Miriam and I dig further.

I opened the folders with monthly statements for payments and pulled out those linked to the deductions in the bank statements. Five different insurance companies and five different policies. I decided the telephone was the quickest way to clarify the situation.

Every policy was to insure David against accidental injury or death. There were NO life insurance policies at all. Two of the policies were quite new, having been taken out in the last twelve months. I was flabbergasted. Why on earth was David paying hundreds (and hundreds) of dollars every month to insure himself against accidental death? Why would he take out new policies after he had been diagnosed with terminal cancer?

Chillingly I remember something David muttered to me, way back when he was first diagnosed and still in his 'angry' stage.

'The best thing that could happen would be if I ran off the road and smashed into a tree on the way home one night,' he had said bitterly. He thought dying in a horrific accident would be preferable to dying slowly of cancer.

At the time I was outraged and told him it was a hideous idea. It was never mentioned again.

Now I am stunned to realise that somewhere in the back of his mind he had continued contemplating this possibility and had taken out additional insurance so that I would benefit from his gruesome death.

This does not console me. It confirms my loathing for everything associated with money and insurance companies and banks and financial institutions. I'm entering my 'angry' stage, furious at a world where such a sinister plot was possible. I cancelled all the policies and was abrupt when speaking to these people. I knew it was not the fault of those dealing with customer relations, but I couldn't seem to help myself.

I also discovered from his credit card statements that David had been buying lottery tickets every week. Quite a few lottery tickets. This astonished me because David had never been a gambler. I can only assume he was trying to pull a rabbit out of a hat, trying to magically acquire a large nest egg so that I would never have to worry about money again. It was all total madness. If he had been killed in an accident (a genuine accident) I would have collected more than a million dollars in insurance payouts. I felt like bull ants were running around inside my head.

Over the next few weeks I had meetings with our lawyer and accountant to try to gain further insight into taking over the management of my life. I did not enjoy any of this. It didn't make me feel powerful or organised or in control. Instead I felt vulnerable and swamped by the complexity of it all. I was also keenly aware that the institutions David had been loyally dealing with for decades felt absolutely no loyalty or moral obligation to help or support me in any way. Regardless of the fact that my income over the preceding twelve years had kept us afloat, I was unable to regain the same level of credit rating or financial support or recognition from any of these institutions after David died. With hindsight I realise this alone would have been a good reason to be involved with money matters while he was alive.

After two weeks, Miriam returns to Adelaide and I'm alone for the first time since David died. I feel lost and slightly dazed. I have very little energy and what little I can muster goes into being his executor, a role in which I'm curiously miscast. David had been concerned that having a lawyer or accountant in this role would cost money. He obviously didn't appreciate how baffling and confronting I would find it.

Bonnie, his dog, is also suffering from grief. Since we adopted her she's spent most of her days trotting along after David. Now he's disappeared. Her sadness manifests itself in confounding attention-getting behaviours like climbing up onto the back of the sofa whenever I sit down, poking me in the neck with her sharp little toenails. She's needy, wanting to be with me every moment and I can't get accustomed to a small black dog jumping onto my lap when I sit on the toilet. If I shut the bathroom door she howls and makes deep claw marks in the timber. Winter's arrived and I find having to go outside into the cold for about twenty minutes every morning so she can pee and poo a shivering ordeal. I think of how any of our labradors would've been if I was sad or upset, gently placing a head in my lap and looking up at me with sorrowful eyes. That's what I need right now, not a dog that wants my undivided attention.

Sid, our cat, on the other hand is maintaining his vigil on David's side of the bed. I'm quite grateful for his company in the middle of the night. It's waking up that I dread the most, because when I'm asleep I forget that David has gone, and when I first open my eyes it all comes flooding back. I long to dream of him; to have him come back to me in sleep, but it doesn't happen. I dream of so many people in my life and so many situations both plausible and surreal – but David never appears. He's vanished from my conscious and subconscious life.

There's always plenty to do around the farm, and I go through the motions of getting the house and garden in order, knowing that I'll probably sell it within the next twelve months. I love the farm and we've been incredibly happy here. I know I won't have the energy or finances to maintain the property and that it could eventually leave me feeling socially isolated.

It suddenly dawns on me that I'm alone – completely alone – for the first time in my life. As a young woman I'd gone from living at home with my family, then briefly in my teens in a share house with my first boyfriend, before falling into a permanent and long-term relationship with David. My mother lived with us for twenty-six years until she died, and all our Leura years were spent with a house overflowing with our children, their friends and various extended family members coming and going. School holidays with all the grandchildren – a busy, crowded, happy life. Now there's just me, a cat and an infuriating dog.

I know my mental state's not good. I sometimes go to yoga in the morning, do some shopping then come back to the farm and spend a few hours on the endless chores associated with such a big property. At some point between one and two in the afternoon I open a bottle of wine and cook myself a late lunch; from there it's downhill all the way. I often sleep for an hour in the late afternoon, get up to feed the animals and check on the poultry and paddock livestock before opening a second bottle of wine and cooking an omelette. I know this isn't healthy or sustainable, but I keep telling myself it's temporary comfort. I believe I'm soothing myself; in reality, I'm making myself numb.

My geographically closest family members – Ethan, Lynne and with their three children – regularly come across from the Blue Mountains to keep an eye on me. This gives me a focus: making a delicious Sunday lunch. I'm greatly cheered by their company. The kids love the farm and we dash around getting kindling before lunch, setting a fire in the dining room then lingering afterwards, talking well into the afternoon. One morning while in the garden a group of three black cockatoos swoop over us and I point them out to Owynn, who is now four years old.

'Look, there goes Granddad,' I say.

'He's alive, he's *alive!*' he gasps. And I feel truly dreadful to have caused this much confusion.

'No, not the real Granddad; his totem,' I lamely explain. I won't make that mistake again.

One weekend Ethan and Lynne initiate a discussion about my plans for the future and Ethan reveals that he discussed where I should live with his father several months before he died. I feel sad that David had been comfortable to discuss my future with our son but not with me. Neither of us had wanted to discuss it; the conversation would have been too painful. It's a regret.

They're proposing to sell the cute cottage they've lived in for eight years and propose that when I've sold the farm, we join forces and buy a place together. To share. I'm amazed and delighted at the proposal, although I worry how such an unusual arrangement might work long term.

We talk it through. We've lived together as an extended family before, when they came to the farm for nearly two years while saving for the deposit on their first house. During that phase we had no problem getting along, sharing the kitchen and living spaces. My children grew up in a family house with a live-in grandmother, so they have no fears about creating a three-generational family. I'd estimated that realistically I could afford to buy a small cottage somewhere nearby and live alone, but this prospect doesn't really appeal to me. It doesn't take me long to decide – I enthusiastically agree to the plan. I'm no longer staring down a black corridor of loneliness. I'll become part of a new extended family. This eases my pain – not completely – but enough to start bringing hope back into my life.

Back at the farm I make a decision I later regret. My yoga group is going on a two-week trip to Bali, and I'm to join them for the second week, when we'll travel by bus to a remote northern village for a peaceful Ayurveda retreat. It's been such a cold winter here at Yetholme, I imagine that the tropical sun and plenty of yoga and resting will do me the world of good. I can't really be away for more than a week because of my limited finances, but also because I'm so involved, almost on a daily basis, with managing David's estate.

My neighbours will keep an eye on the farm – and the animals including the cat, but Bonnie the pug is a problem because she's so insecure and demanding and really needs someone around twenty-four hours a day. I don't think a dog kennel will work for her either, so I phone the woman from the pug rescue organisation she came from eighteen months ago. I ask if they provide respite care for these situations, and I also explain how difficult I'm finding it trying to keep her happy since David died. I describe some of her extreme behaviours and how inconsolable she is if she's separated from me.

'Ah,' the rescue woman says knowingly. 'She's a velcro pug.' A pug that needs to be permanently attached, she explains.

It seems that some of the more highly-strung pugs, especially black females, exhibit these behaviours. I'm not alone!

She then offers a suggestion that shocks me: 'I think you'd be happier and Bonnie would be happier if we find her a home where it isn't a one-on-one relationship. Dogs like Bonnie can be exhausting and she'll be better housed with a family – perhaps with some children and other dogs to keep her company.'

What she's saying makes perfect sense, but I feel I'll be betraying David if I give up on this little dog that he loved so much. I talk it over with my family and they all agree with the rescue worker. They know all too well how much Bonnie's wearing me down, and they think it's a practical and emotionally sensible decision.

I drive Bonnie to Sydney, crying all the way. I do love her, but I know that we're a complete mismatch at this stage in my life. I can barely manage my own grief, let alone hers. We meet in a park. The rescue woman (who endearingly looks a bit like a pug herself) gives Bonnie a big kiss on the nose and I hand her over. I feel wretched.

Several days later a message and photo come through on my phone. Bonnie is pictured with two other pugs, cuddled up and smiling. The message says they have found a fantastic family for her, with three children and plenty of action to keep her distracted and busy. I feel huge relief, but also very sad that I couldn't be a better companion for this small vulnerable animal. Cats are easier, more independent. I might never have another dog.

Arriving at the airport for the week in Bali, I check my bag in and make my way through immigration and security into the duty-free hall. Then it hits me. This is the moment when I usually settle myself with a cup of tea or a glass of wine and phone David to let him know that everything has gone smoothly and to plan. He always wanted to know that I was okay; that there had been no delays or complications. I stare at my mobile phone. There's nobody to call. No point phoning the children; they'll all be rushing to work and getting on with their busy lives. The emptiness I feel at this moment is indescribable. Is this how grief works, I wonder. Everything goes along as normal, then suddenly reality hits?

Bali is hot and sweaty and Ubud full of Australian tourists. I'm pleased we'll be heading for a more remote region of the island the following day.

What I hadn't realised about the retreat is that, as well as morning and evening yoga, the daily itinerary includes three or more 'pampering' treatments. I quite like a massage but I would probably only have one a year at most. I simply don't crave it – or facials or foot rubs or deep baths with fragrant oils. It all seems like a lot of fuss to me and I'd rather be walking or reading or gardening.

My first massage is an ordeal. I have a shower and dress in a bathrobe then am ushered into a delightful room with tinkling chimes, soft music and fragrant candles. Lying naked on the massage table I place my face in the cosy hole provided, and see a gorgeous bowl of tropical blooms directly below me. The lovely young woman who will massage me speaks softly as she prepares warm oils. The moment she touches my back with deep circular movements, it opens a floodgate of sobs. It's the intimacy of a hand on my skin that releases such an overwhelming and devastating sense of loss. My tears cascade into the flowers under the table, and I tremble with anguish. I haven't expected this, and the poor young woman doesn't know what to do. I ask her to stop, apologise and dash to the safety of my room.

I'm not ready to be so far from home so soon after losing David, and the next six days can't go fast enough. I manage to have a few treatments but don't find them soothing. The yoga is good, though very sweaty, I spend most of my time hiding and reading – it's too hot and sticky to go for long walks – and I do manage to get some sleep. It's a lesson learned the hard way. You can't run away from your sadness. Better to stay close to home and process it than believe escape to a tropical island will help ease the pain.

The farmhouse is bitterly cold and cheerless when I return from the tropics and I do my best to lift my mood by lighting two fires – one in the kitchen cooker and one in the family room where David and I spent so much time over the last two years. There's plenty of firewood in the shed but I do need to drive into town for supplies – fresh fruit and vegetables, there's not much growing in the garden this time of the year, and most importantly, more wine.

It's time to take stock of the animals. In the main paddock I have a few sheep, including a magnificent Dorper ram, two alpacas and a small herd of goats. Maybe ten. Both the female goats are pregnant; both look like they're carrying twins. Then there are seven chickens and a rooster. I'll need to find homes for the livestock when I sell up. I'll miss calling out to them from the kitchen window every morning and seeing them gather at the fence knowing that I'll soon come out with some treats. Leafy greens from the vegetable garden and stale crusts of bread. They're affectionate creatures and I love them.

I try not to think of these proposed changes as 'loss'. I know that my life's been rich with a large loving family and a wonderful home with space to make beautiful gardens and keep animals. The loss of David has been my greatest hurt, but I'll also miss these surroundings and this tranquil way of life. I just have to be positive and think about my future in a different way. It's about moving forward. I will still have my treks in the mountains, my children and grandchildren, and now also the excitement of looking for a house to share with my youngest son and his lovely family.

Aaron has work scheduled in this region for six weeks, so is staying with me at the farm from Monday to Friday. The difference it makes having another person in the house; someone to cook for and talk to about the nightly television news! It's a bit pointless railing against the antics of politicians when you're on your own. He's also helped me get some important jobs done around the farm, but it's midwinter and we lose light so early it doesn't leave much time for chores. He leaves very early every morning, before daybreak.

The last week of his stay seems like good time to fly to Adelaide, see my daughter and grandsons and pick up David's car for the long drive home. I want to sell it before the annual registration is due, and Aaron's there at the farm every evening to keep an eye on the animals while I'm away for five days. In the past I always took it for granted that David would be around to hold the fort whenever I travelled with my groups to France and the Himalayas. It's yet another bonus of our planned extended family living, to know that I'll be able to just walk out and shut the bedroom door and my cat will be fed and the pot plants watered.

I enjoy long drives on my own. It's the ultimate in personal space, being in a car bubble with just the music playing and the scenery of Australia all around. The long drive home from Adelaide to Renmark and Mildura, then on to Hay in far western New South Wales is seasonally beautiful, with vineyards and neat fields in quiet dormancy. The architecture of the rural towns in South Australia is so different from New South Wales, with shops and houses of the dark local stone. I drive all day and stop in the remote township of Hay overnight. After sitting in front of a steering wheel for hours I need to move, so I go for a long walk around the town after dinner. I sleep well.

I leave extremely early, hoping to get home to the farm by mid-afternoon. People can be disparaging about driving across the Hay Plain, saying it's boring and flat – a dull and featureless landscape. My reaction to this place is the opposite. I cherish this long and lonely drive, with the horizon shimmering in the distance, and the roadside lined with tufts of native grasses. Sections are treeless, but never desolate to my eye. Just outside Hay, as the sun's starting to break through, I come upon a vast herd of cattle covering the entire road. I know the drought last summer left many farmers without sufficient feed to get their stock through the winter. I've seen on the news that some are slowly droving their animals to market early, allowing them to fatten up on the grazing that's still available along the sides of the road. The long paddock. I've never witnessed a sight like this before and I find it quite thrilling in the early morning light; this sea of animals with stockmen herding them very slowly around my stationary car. I turn off the engine, wind the window down a little and just watch, enthralled. The smell of crisp early morning mingled with the sharp scent of cattle fills the car. To my left I see a campsite being packed up; with four-wheel drives and caravans. A breakfast fire is being extinguished. One young man on horseback comes alongside my car, leans down and waves to me through the side window, smiling broadly. I'm ecstatic. I realise it's a romanticised view of Australian country life, and I know that historically life and conditions for stockmen have a brutal and racist history. However, the visual impact of it is dazzling, and after the herd passes me I drive away on a high.

I have lunch in Cowra and just as I'm motoring out of town Aaron phones to see how I'm going. I tell him my location and ask after Sid, as he didn't eat his breakfast on the morning I left for Adelaide.

He hesitates and then tells me that he found Sid dead in the shed the previous morning. He had no marks on his body, and no evidence of snake bite. He's already buried him.

The shock of this news scarily triggers a grief I hadn't experienced before – even when I was at my lowest ebb on the massage table in Bali. I continue driving, even more anxious to get home as quickly as possible. I'm howling like a madwoman, sobbing and screaming a primal wail from somewhere deep inside. I'm driving fast – very fast – between each town, hoping the highway patrols are not out this afternoon. After being fined for speeding I would be taken immediately to a psychiatric ward under lock and key. I'm completely out of control. Normally it's nearly a two-hour drive but I do it in less. I vaguely regain composure about fifteen minutes before reaching the farm. I'm totally drained and disorientated when I finally get home. Aaron isn't there – it's Friday and he's heading back to Mudgee for the weekend. He's not aware of my mental state.

The house is unwelcoming. No Sid and I'd given Bonnie away. I crawl into bed and sleep for hours, waking in the dark, hungry and in need of a drink.

I light the fire, make an omelette and put on some music. Although still exhausted, I also feel a strange lightness. A release. As though my unrestrained crying has expelled some demons held within me. I've tried so hard to control my emotions because I don't want to upset other people, especially my children and grandchildren. I've held onto my pain and my sadness and simply gone through the motions of getting going with my life: organising a painter to come and spruce up the farmhouse; finalising the details of David's will; making important financial decisions for my future. I have no doubt that being inside a car, a sealed and private capsule, allowed me the freedom to finally let it all out. To scream and bash the steering wheel in a frenzied fury. It would seem that David wasn't the only one to be angry about death.

35

Feeling my way

THE FARM, SEPTEMBER 2014

The warm sunny days heading into spring lift my spirits. The vivid green of the first leaf bursts on the deciduous trees, the showy pink and white cherry blossom and the tiny purple crocus and golden hoop petticoat narcissus. Springtime renewal always lifts my spirits after the seemingly never-ending freezing winter. Never have I more craved my mood to soar.

The younger of the nanny goats produces perfect twins one frosty morning, and I cobble together a small covered enclosure at the back of the poultry shed so they are warm at night while I keep a close eye on them. She happily allows me to handle the kids, cuddling them and giving them cute names. I take lots of photographs and email them to the grandchildren.

Symbols of regeneration are strong and heartening.

The older of the nannies also goes into labour. She's had four births in her time here with us, but I'm uncertain of her previous history. This time she's really struggling, lying down for several hours and making no progress. I sit with her and wait. She allows me to stroke her head but during contractions she's pawing at the ground and moaning deeply. I've never seen her distressed like this before.

I consult my laptop, googling 'goat birth'. She fits the criteria of a mother goat in trouble and needing help, so I check out a couple of YouTube clips of goat farmers assisting their animals at birth. It doesn't seem that daunting and I decide to try to help her before resorting to the vet.

After the homebirth of my last child I spent a few years working side by side with our local midwife who was doing births in the upper Blue Mountains. I'm not afraid of birth and really enjoyed this period my life, working with families in their homes and sharing the thrill of each new arrival. I regard birth as a pretty normal, natural and generally uncomplicated event and I'm certain that for animals it should be even more so.

As directed by YouTube, I cut my fingernails very short and scrub my hands clean. No gloves, they say, as you can feel what is happening better with bare fingers. I slip my hand inside her and can feel the sharp little hooves and the kid's forehead in the correct position. With my laptop replaying the clip at my side, I follow the directions exactly. Gently I manipulate the hooves downwards during each contraction, to support her natural pushing momentum. I can see that the head's in the correct position and, with the next big push, the glistening little creature emerges unscathed, breathing immediately, even struggling to its wobbly feet.

The nanny stands and attends to her newborn as I'd hoped. It suckles briefly then she goes down again. There's a second kid. She's exhausted, so I feel again for the hooves and again I help her – very gently, very slowly – to bring her offspring into the world. Everything works as it should. The placentas are normal, the kids both active. I make a warm place for them with straw bales and blankets on the back veranda and feed the mother with pellets. Next morning they are all strong enough to graze in the sunny paddock.

It feels so good to experience a little joy and hope again. I bond with those kids and they follow me around the garden. I let them come into the kitchen, laughing to imagine how horrified David would have been at young goats trying to bounce onto the breakfast table. They are adorable.

My contentment is short-lived. I've been having some painting and maintenance done inside the farmhouse and it's all beginning to come together. I'm imagining that by the middle of summer I'll be ready to put the property onto the market, perhaps sometime after Christmas.

But there's a dramatic change in the weather during late spring, with high winds and a severe drop in temperature. I put the mother goats and their kids into the large poultry shed as I fear we're in for a snowy night. Waking very early to chilling silence, I pull back the curtains and see that deep snow surrounds the house. The trees lining the driveway, already in leaf, have collapsed under the sheer weight of the snow and branches and trunks cover the road, making it impossible to drive in and out of the farm. In the back garden it's even worse. The massive tree, the central feature of the back garden, has split down the middle and given way. Fences and the poultry enclosure have been knocked down and the whole place looks like a bomb has been dropped on it. It will take weeks to clear up the havoc that's occurred in just a few hours.

This is a major setback to my plans. I need the gardens and the paddocks to look lush and well-tended before I can realistically advertise the farm for sale. I am, momentarily, defeated. It's a harsh reminder that I really can't stay at the farm and manage huge problems like this on my own.

Apart from the storm, the sale of the farm needs to be delayed as I've decided to keep the five acres that's across the road but still part of the title deed. It's an odd-shaped block with lots of rogue pine trees that have self-sown from the state forest at nearby Sunny Corner. We always loved walking through this deeply wooded acreage, which is rich with birdlife and home to wallabies and wild rabbits. As David is now buried in the historic graveyard, I feel reluctant to just sell up and disappear from the hamlet. I believe that if I can hang onto this little slice of our paradise I'll maintain a connection. I even fantasise about building a yurt there, having fallen in love with this ancient nomadic structure during a botanical trek in Mongolia.

Again, I'm out of my depth, naive about the intricacies of subdivision. What I've imagined to be a straightforward procedure turns out to involve a lot of time and expense – I need to have the entire property surveyed with new boundaries drawn up; I need environmental impact studies, soil-testing – all sorts of red tape to wade through. With help I draw up a timeline that indicates it won't be until the following spring that I will be 100 per cent certain of having the farmhouse and the remaining twenty acres available for auction. I can just about financially afford the cost of the subdivision and the delay in selling, but I'm fearful about having another ten to twelve months of living alone.

My son and daughter-in-law aren't overly concerned as this will give them additional time to renovate their cottage before putting it on the market. We decide not to even look at prospective houses until we're all closer to being able to sell.

Miriam phones often from Adelaide to keep tabs on me. She has such a busy and vibrant life and our conversations are peppered with newsy stories about her four growing sons and tales from her exacting workplace. We both love to reminisce about her childhood and the time when her own children were very young, but she still gets very weepy whenever she talks about her father. She misses him deeply. It's going to take a long time for all of us to get through the pain.

During one call she mentions that her eldest son, Eamonn, has finished a TAFE course and isn't sure which direction to take next. Work's very difficult to find for young people in South Australia, and he's spent weeks and weeks applying for jobs without success. He wants to save up so he can get driving lessons and buy a car.

'Send him to me,' I suggest, half kidding. 'I'll teach him to drive and he can help me to get a lot of things done around the farm. It'll give him time to think about his future.'

She jumps at the idea, but needs to check with him. Eamonn readily agrees and I'm thrilled at the prospect of his company for several months at least. He arrives with all his electronic gadgets and sets up in one of the spare bedrooms.

Eamonn has his first lesson with a driving school vehicle then I let him drive us back to the farm in my manual four-wheel drive ute. I'm absolutely terrified during these first few drives together, but he seems to have a natural knack and I quickly became more at ease. It's quite a fun thing for us to do together, and I feel his confidence grow as the spring turns into summer.

I also teach him the fundamentals of operating the tractor and he enjoys taking it out, mowing the lawns and slashing the paddocks. He loves the animals and happily helps me with a whole range of routine chores including castrating the male kids. He does some external house painting, some of the never-ending plumbing repairs and helps the surveyor by making sure he can identify all the peculiar corners of the property. Having Eamonn around is such a pleasure – he has a voracious appetite and it's so much fun to cook for him. It gives me a sense of purpose.

The next obstacle to get through is Christmas. I couldn't imagine a Christmas without David, so we're planning something completely different – a lunch with Lynne's family in the Blue Mountains. It feels very strange, dressing up for a Christmas lunch that I won't be cooking myself. I'm hoping that, in a completely different setting, I can disassociate from it. Eamonn does the driving and this is also a weird experience. I've never been out on the road on Christmas morning and am amazed at the volume of traffic. This mass movement of people all heading to family gatherings.

I try to feel like I'm part of it; I'm indeed very much part of this welcoming extended family. But this annual celebration has always pivoted around our home and my preparations. It's just another adjustment I need to make as part of my new life. A new order. I drink a lot of champagne.

36

Time for something new

My plan after Christmas is to return to France. After all these years I have such mixed feelings about this place because of everything that's gone before. When I first open the door and enter the beautiful main room with the massive fireplace, the familiar smell of old stone and wood fire alone evokes so many memories, both good and bad. I always throw open the shutters and let sunlight stream in through the huge arched front windows onto the wide polished floorboards. Then I open the small shutter-and-glass door onto the courtyard and never fail to be moved by the beauty of the ancient stone-work facade of the barn. It has the original timber doors, although they're slowly crumbling. I remember our joy when we first bought this place and our plans for making it our own special retreat. We didn't spend a fortune – we couldn't afford to – however we managed to install a lovely kitchen and when Ethan and Lynne came over for six months, they gave everything a fresh coat of paint. Over the years I've added many personal touches – paintings, comfortable chairs, books and a collection of CDs. I feel very much at home here and quickly reconnect with my circle of friends.

The sad times associated with this place are mostly connected to the affair I had when I was here on my own. The pain that it caused has tainted my feelings about myself and my relationship with this country. Although it's ancient history now, it still comes back to haunt me, especially since David died. Several other close friends who I knew when we first came to France have also died, and this brings me great sadness as well. The knowledge that life cannot remain the same forever. It seems to be a constant process of letting go.

The main reason for coming to France this time is to notify the authorities that David has died and begin the complex business of the 'succession', which is the French term for inheritance. We hadn't made wills in France and therefore I had to follow the somewhat antiquated law that favours the children, often at the disadvantage of the spouse. The house is not worth much, indeed it's barely increased in value in the fifteen years since we bought it. I organise a meeting with the notaire, the local legal official who did all the paperwork when we purchased the property all those years ago.

I hand her the death certificate and she explains what needs to be done. The house is in both our names and so I'm allowed to keep my half, then as David's wife I inherit half of his half. The rest is to be divided between our four children. The hitch is that when I die my percentage of the property can only be inherited by my three biological children which disadvantages David's son Tony – the oldest child. I try to debate the issue with the notaire, pointing out that under our Australian wills the four children will inherit equally when I eventually die.

'He is not your blood,' she repeats several times. I find it all very strange. In France you cannot disinherit a child and if a man fathers a child outside his marriage, that child is also entitled to an equal share of the inheritance. It creates dramas all over France as families squabble and houses remain unoccupied for decades while the children fight about what should be done. It all sounds fair on paper, but in reality it's a social nightmare.

I make the decision to gift my share of the house to our children immediately, to avoid these future dramas. I can't imagine my kids falling out over a cottage of such small value on the other side of the world, but you never know. I was really trying to simplify my life as much as possible. I'll happily continue to visit the house every year and pay the local taxes, and I hope our children and grandchildren will all soon be in a financial position where they can start using the house themselves. I'm certain the grandchildren would benefit greatly from spending some time in France.

I have many friends in France, but I still sometimes manage to feel quite lonely. There's always a lot of socialising – lunches, dinners, markets, walks – but essentially, I'm on my own. For many years I have come to France without David to lead village walking tours and these have been tremendous fun and a great way for me to learn even more about this remote rural corner of the world. On the tours we walk in the mornings through woods and little hamlets, have a sumptuous lunch in a village and then go by bus to fabulous gardens and chateaux. The evenings are spent enjoying the very best of the local cuisine and wines. I've always wanted my tours to be affordable and accessible to a wide range of travellers, not just the wealthy, but with the rise of the euro and the fall in the Australian dollar these tours have become increasingly expensive.

Now that David's gone I have a strong feeling that I must do something quite different on this side of the world. I'm not sure why, but because my life has changed so dramatically I sense that my work here also needs to shift and evolve. Since his death I'm simply not the same person. I need new challenges and new destinations to define myself. I didn't like the idea of just carrying on with the 'old' as if nothing's happened. I need a fresh perspective on my life.

I look southwards to Morocco. I've always wanted to see this country but it hasn't been on my radar despite being only a short flight from Toulouse to Casablanca or Marrakech – and Toulouse being just a short train trip from my nearest big town. So why not?

I talk to my colleagues at World Expeditions in Sydney and discover they have an association with a Marrakech-based travel group which organises trips for Australians. As it's low season, they offer to show me around and help me plan an itinerary for possible future tours. I have a friend from Canada staying with me at the house and she wants to tag along and look at Morocco as well, so we book return flights and the Moroccan travel company recommends a fabulous riad – a traditional house with a courtyard – inside the ancient walls of the city. I pinch myself: I'm actually going to do this!

People have sometimes said to me that they think I'm brave and that I've said 'Yes' to difficult challenges and jumped at opportunities that they would have found daunting. I was lulled into believing the myth that I was fearless until David died and I recognised that it was he who gave me permission to be daring. He'd always been my great support, cheering me on when I launched myself into something different and demanding. He was only ever a phone call away, and he rescued me on numerous occasions when I went in over my depth. He applauded my successes and comforted me if I fell on my face. He was content to stay behind the scenes, handling the business and administrative side of my adventures. Now somehow I have to be brave without him. Morocco will be my first big test.

On this first trip, simply the route from the airport into Marrakech takes my breath away – I'm not sure what I was expecting, but not this. Neatly landscaped avenues of palms and lushly flowering shrubs; orderly traffic flow and the most brilliant of blue cloudless skies. As we glimpse the old walls of the city my heart's beating fast. It feels so exotic but not in any way daunting. People are bustling about their business and I love the sight of men wearing long djellabas with pointed hoods. I also notice many young women, their heads uncovered and driving scooters or sitting in sidewalk cafés drinking coffee. So different from Kashmir where young women are virtually invisible.

We enter through an ancient fortified gateway and into the medina, the old city. We drive down a narrow street between high walls and stop next to a simple but beautiful arched wooden door. Our guide presses a buzzer and a woman opens the heavy door, smiling. Within moments we enter the riad via a narrow corridor that that turns sharp right and then left. Suddenly we're in a marvellous courtyard, open to the sky with three storeys and a narrow winding staircase that we discover leads to the roof terrace and garden. From the outside on the street, there was no indication of the beauty that lies within. We're served exquisite glasses of mint tea, poured ceremoniously from a silver teapot, and some delicious sweet biscuits. Inside, the riad is a feast for the eyes – comfortable sofas with plump silk cushions, elegant brass light fittings and lamps, colourful handwoven rugs and ornate wall mosaics. We've arrived.

Our local guide describes the Moroccan houses as having been built 'inside out', with balconies on the inside surrounding the central courtyard. Given the extremes of the climate, especially in summer, this makes such good sense as the courtyards remain cool and protected from the summer sun, yet provide excellent air circulation. He tells us that Muslims avoid external displays of wealth, preferring houses – rich or poor – to appear very much the same from the street. Just a simple door.

There's so much to take in – visually and mentally. We hit the road, driving to Rabat on the coast, with its ancient fortification (kasbah) and Roman ruins; Meknes, which has a French-built new town with brilliantly preserved Art Deco architecture; Fes, one of the oldest continuously inhabited Muslim cities in the world, with a World Heritage-listed medina and wonderful architecture and souks; the astounding Roman ruins of Volubulis and finally back to Marrakech with its famous open square, Jemaa el-Fnaa, a bustling marketplace with snake charmers, dancers and other exotic entertainers. Visiting the souks – undercover markets in the medina – in every city is like stepping into another world.

An unexpected treasure I discover on my last day is the Majorelle Garden. I go alone without high expectations because some friends in France had said they didn't find it impressive. It's such a thrill when you're not expecting much and stumble into something extraordinary. The original house and garden were built by the French artist Jacques Majorelle in the 1930s when Morocco was a French protectorate. The house is Cubist in design – I've never seen anything like it. Majorelle was a passionate amateur botanist and he laid the foundations of the unforgettable walled dry-climate garden that is now permanently open to the public. In the 1980s the property was bought by fashion designer Yves Saint Laurent and his partner Pierre Bergé, who restored both the house

and garden and introduced a dramatic colour scheme domi-
nated by cobalt blue.

I wander slowly through this oasis, taking it all in. It encap-
sulates how I feel about this entire country: surprise, delight
and fascination. I have no doubt I'll be back with a group,
so I spend several hours in the late afternoon fine-tuning a
proposed itinerary for a tour the following year. I decide to
include several days in a Berber village in the High Atlas
Mountains in central Morocco with some day walks, even
though I haven't had time to travel up to that region on
this reconnaissance visit. Next time! For eight precious days
I haven't felt sad or adrift or solitary. My future, I realise,
must surely lie in adventure.

37

Home again

Back in Australia my mood plummets, so I decide to try grief counselling. I know this service is offered by the cancer clinic where David had his chemo and I'd briefly met the counsellor, but I never imagined I'd ever need this intervention.

I'm entitled to seven one-hour sessions – more if the counsellor believes I still have unresolved issues. I have no idea what this process will involve but she immediately makes me feel at ease, sitting comfortably on a deep sofa. We talk openly. It goes like this: she prompts me with a couple of leading questions and my thoughts and feelings just tumble out of my mouth. It's a balm to have someone neutral to talk to. I haven't wanted to bang on about David's death to friends and family. To me, it feels like burdening other people with my own private angst. I'd rather put on a brave face and afterwards drink a bottle of wine than risk boring someone witless with my seemingly petty gripes. Most people have experienced a death; most people know about loss. Why should my grief be any more of an ordeal than for anyone else?

At the second session the counsellor sums up what we discussed the previous week. She describes my condition as 'complicated grief' because David's death happened so dramatically and with a lot of trauma. In my heart, I must have known that David was going to die but I'd pushed it somewhere off into the future. I hadn't expected him to lose cognitive function or disappear so quickly.

The counsellor also believes that David's rage about dying, his lack of acceptance, made things tough for those around him, having to deal with a sick person who's also angry.

The one-hour sessions go quickly. I have plenty to say and the counsellor is subjected weekly to my tangled stream of thoughts. I talk about the last consultation with the oncologist and my inability to communicate clearly at that crucial meeting my concerns about David's laboured breathing. I accept that it wouldn't have made any difference to the outcome in the long term, but I'm upset with myself for not advocating for him more clearly. I talk about my fear of being alone and of hating being responsible for my own financial security. I talk about not having those final conversations with David because of his delirium. No proper goodbye. No resolution. Most of all, I talk about the sleepless nights, when I'm jolted awake because my warm foot has accidentally strayed against the icy-cold sheets on the empty side of the bed. The desolation.

Sometimes, I just cry.

The counsellor organises a post-mortem consultation with the specialist. It makes me feel better, just expressing to him what's been troubling me about David's last consultation. She suggests I leave the electric blanket on a low setting on David's side of the bed, so I'm no longer shocked awake by the frigid reminder of my solitude. She encourages me to write down all the things I need to say to David, to express them in a tangible form.

I also go to see our GP, who was also rattled about David's swift demise. He diagnoses depression – what he calls 'reactive depression', brought about by a sudden change of circumstances: an accident, an injury, a death. He prescribes a mild antidepressant which he believes, if taken in the evening, will also help me to sleep more calmly. The label says to avoid driving and alcohol so I half-heartedly reduce – but don't eliminate – my glasses of wine in the evening.

After starting these meds I sleep deeply – a drugged but peaceful sleep. I'm slightly fuzzy during the day, but still able to function and gradually, over the next two weeks, I start to feel a little less anxious. A little less pessimistic. I'm dismayed to find myself in this situation, needing drugs and counselling. I hope to eventually wean myself off these props by the time I move from here to my new life in the mountains.

'Empathy' has only been in common usage for perhaps the last ten or fifteen years. Previously, words like 'sympathy', 'pity' and 'compassion' were used to describe how we felt and reacted to another person's bereavement or loss. Empathy is modern jargon and it implies that we are somehow capable of putting ourselves into the shoes of the person who is suffering. I can't see how this is realistic or achievable.

Over the last few decades several of our friends have lost their life partners and when it happened I really believed I understood how that might feel. I thought I could empathise. One of David's oldest and closest friends from New Zealand came to visit us not long before he died. This friend had recently lost his wife of more than fifty years and during his visit he seemed to me like a different person. His body language and mannerisms – the way he walked and talked – had altered. It was much more than just gradual ageing. He didn't laugh as much and sometimes he just went very quiet, as if in another world.

Only now can I understand that his grief was so intense it had changed who he was. He simply didn't present as the same person.

I get it. That's what empathy means: understanding and insight. Perhaps we can only truly empathise when the same situation has befallen us. I've never lost a child and while I can try to imagine how that might feel I simply cannot truly understand the depth of the pain it would evoke. How can I comprehend the feelings of a refugee locked up for a decade in an offshore detention centre or step into the shoes of an ageing homeless woman living in an old car parked in a back street or how it feels to have been sexually molested as a child? Only now can I empathise with David's old friend from New Zealand.

I am part of a new tribe: the widowed. I haven't just lost David, I've lost a slice of who I am. Part of my identity. When I get up in the morning I'm living a different life. The patterns and routines of my day have changed. I make my own tea and toast and take it back to bed, alone. I no longer need to consider David. It feels very strange indeed.

Some people see this new phase as a fresh start; a new beginning. I had an aunt whose husband hated air travel and every year they put their car on the train from Sydney to Tweed Heads where they rented the same holiday house for nearly five decades. This lack of adventure must have been galling, because within months of his death my aunt, well into her eighties, took off and flew. She hopped on and off planes until she'd seen all of Australia and even New Zealand. Her husband's death had given her wings. Liberated her.

I can still enjoy my life and always manage to have fun wherever I go. But it's a different life and I'm a different woman. Not any more sober or settled; just different.

38

An extreme adventure

LADAKH, MAY 2015

The need for new destinations and fresh experiences leads me to arrange a yoga trip to Ladakh, high in the mountains of northern India and close to both the Kashmir and Tibetan borders. One of my regular local guides, Narwang, lives in this remote and beautiful part of the world and he's often suggested that I'd love it. Now seems like the perfect time to visit.

It's great this time to have a few blokes in the group because often yoga trips end up being female-only expeditions. One man, a regular at our yoga studio, has brought his teenage son along and a woman has inveigled her husband into joining us. Later we'll be so grateful that these men came along with us.

Few people have heard of Ladakh and I certainly knew nothing about it until I met Narwang. It has a complex story with evidence of habitation dating back to Neolithic times and a long history of invasions and takeovers, treachery, powerful royal families and ferocious armies. It was a strategic stopover on the rich trading routes through the Himalayas and has a mixed population of Sunni Muslims (from the Pakistan and Kashmir side), Tibetan Buddhists, and a much smaller number of Hindus and Sikhs. An agreement was signed to join Ladakh to India at the end of British rule (Partition in 1947) yet to this day it simply doesn't feel like India to me – it feels like a world apart. A mesmerising hidden treasure.

It's always been difficult to get to the capital, Leh, which is nestled in the Indus Valley surrounded by high passes. It took days to navigate these wild and high-altitude roads until the Indian air force installed a strategic landing strip that now also serves as the main airport, bringing people in and out for most months of the year. The roads are completely unpassable during late autumn and winter.

Planes can only take off and land in the early morning as the mountain winds that whip up during the day make the journey perilous. Our group arrives in Delhi the afternoon before our flight to Leh and we have a briefing before a very early night, to be ready for our 3am wake up calls for the 5am flight. After take-off, we can't see much through the thick haze that surrounds Delhi but as we set our course to the mountains the air clears and the spectacular scenery of the Himalayan foothills unfolds below us, lush with dense forest and river systems. Suddenly we're above the tree line and floating over impressive snow-capped craggy mountains.

The landing is smooth and as we disembark the mountains completely wrap around us. I notice people turning in circles, mouths wide open. We also start to feel a little light-headed as the altitude takes hold. We've travelled from an altitude of 230 metres in Delhi to 3500 metres in under two hours. It will take several days to acclimatise.

Our charming hotel is in the distinctive architectural style of the region, with white-painted exterior walls and ornately carved and decorated dark timber window and door frames. It has a beautiful courtyard garden with views to the mountains. As we are welcomed with tea and little sweet cakes, I notice in the foyer two oxygen bottles with face masks – for people badly affected by altitude sickness. Roughly half of the group are taking Diamox, a medication that alleviates the symptoms. I've decided against it, having read that it 'masks' symptoms and can produce a false sense of well-being when the body is struggling to cope with less oxygen. For each trekker it has to be a personal decision. Although it's still early and we're excited and curious to explore, most head for their beds to lie down, trying to acclimatise. Everyone's affected differently by the change in altitude, which can strike down the youngest and fittest member of a group. We have headaches of varying degrees and can't believe how difficult it is to just climb a small flight of stairs – puffing and panting with heavy legs. After a simple lunch we rest again for several hours before attempting a gentle walk around the town and a short hike up to the Buddhist Shanti Stupa, which rewards us with panoramic views of the entire river valley and the city. Exhausted, we barely talk at dinner, and have another early night.

Over the next two days our bodies adapt to the conditions. Each day we do more exploring, visiting monasteries and ancient villages, and by day four we are leaping up the stairs easily – which is just as well because tomorrow we'll start our trek up and over several high passes – one of them more than 5000 metres above sea level. On most days we will be trekking for at least 6–7 hours, and longer if the terrain is difficult.

Our first day of walking is not too strenuous, although we do feel the heat of walking through terrain with little or no vegetation or canopy. Ladakh is an alpine desert with a minuscule amount of annual rainfall. At this altitude there are some shrubs and smaller plants along the banks of the rivers and streams, and denser woodland in the folds between the hills and mountains but otherwise it's a dry and barren landscape. Spectacular colours layer the rocky cliffs, from deep purples and reds through to cream and silver. You can almost see how these mountains were formed layer by layer over millions and millions of years. In the last hour before reaching our camp, some in the group seem very hot and tired – I can always tell by the way we're walking. Exhausted trekkers are inclined to stumble and trip and we all seem a little wobbly on our feet. We've come a long way and are still obviously feeling the effects of the altitude.

It's a wonderful feeling when you see that circle of orange tents in the distance, knowing the kettle will be on for a late afternoon pot of tea. Our tents and sleeping mats will offer welcome respite. While we're enjoying our tea the weather suddenly changes, with dark clouds approaching and the temperature dropping dramatically. I notice a lot of excited chatter among the porters, guides and cooks who are glancing at the sky and packing things away. Then two men with shovels start digging trenches around our tents while others are rounding up the pack animals which had been released to graze around the campsite.

Our head guide tells me they fear a cloudburst is imminent. It's not a term that meteorologists use in Australia, preferring 'a sudden heavy rain event'. It describes that moment when, in a matter of minutes, almost an entire year's rainfall comes down in a huge, dangerous dump. Not too concerned, we go on drinking tea until quite suddenly the skies open. We make for our tents. I can barely hear anything over the sound of the rain pelting down. There's a lot of scurrying, the scratch of digging and the occasional shriek. Then the rain ceases as dramatically as it started and I peek outside to see rivers of mud surrounding us. The bedraggled crew have been entirely saturated while they furiously tried diverting the water and mud from the tents. The trekkers seem fine, however several of the tents are wet and muddy inside.

The following day will prove to be the longest and hardest in all my years of trekking. What we don't realise when we're cheerfully eating our breakfast after dawn yoga practice is that the cloudburst has created huge obstacles for us in the terrain ahead. The plan today is to slowly ascend to just over 5000 metres at Khandungla Pass where we'll begin our downhill trek to the mighty Indus River. Here we'll be collected by jeeps and taken to our comfy hotel in the ancient village of Alchi. The sun's shining brightly as we set off, however it isn't very hot, which is a great relief: there'll be little or no shade.

Naturally we fall into three groups – the fast walkers with the lead guide, the middle group who keep a steady pace and then the stragglers. I like to walk with the third group to keep their spirits up when the going gets tough. Our lungs are feeling the altitude with every step. Those taking Diamox appear less affected but even so, everyone is moving quite slowly with frequent stops to oxygenise. The track zigzags along and I've lost sight of the fast walkers until I round a bend and see a pocket of lush greenery ahead, a stark contrast to the bare rocks we've been seeing all morning. As we get closer I can see a herd of animals grazing and closer still I recognise wild yaks – the dominant male is easily the largest and most impressive yak I've ever seen. His horns are colossal. There are at least eight calves in colours varying from white through shades of red brown to black. It's a breathtaking sight I've never witnessed before. Then I see that someone's walking through the herd and realise with horror that it's Glenda, a delightful woman from Melbourne who's obviously being a little too adventurous for her own safety.

'Glenda!' I shout and she turns to see me motioning furiously at her to get away from such potentially dangerous animals. She completely ignores me and keeps mingling with the yaks and taking photographs.

Eventually, struggling to breathe, I get to a level where

I can see she's moving away from the herd and out of danger. I'm quite shaken, given the implications of what could've happened if she'd been gored by the protective wild male, who could weigh up to 1000 kilos. Glenda's smiling broadly but her face falls when she sees my stern expression.

I make it a rule never to get angry with my trekkers, but this time I just can't contain my emotions.

'Why the hell didn't you get away from the herd when I called you?' I ask through gritted teeth.

'I just wanted to get a close-up of the white yak sitting down,' she says. 'I've never seen a white yak before.'

'You can download a bloody photo of a white yak from the internet,' I say with exasperation. 'It's a safer option.'

I explain that had she been injured or killed it would've impacted dramatically on every single person in the group, from the local guides to her fellow trekkers. We're at least one full day, or even more, away from any transport to seek medical assistance. It could have been a major disaster.

Glenda looks crestfallen and accepts that she was foolish to put herself in that situation. My heart's still beating wildly but I signal to the lead guide to recommence walking. In my fright I don't even take a photograph of the yak herd. Ironically, I'll probably have to ask Glenda to send me one of her pics.

Even though I'm not singularly responsible for people on these treks, I take their safety very seriously. I want everyone to have an incredible and positive experience, but I always want to minimise the hazards. As a general rule avoiding close contact with animals is standard for travellers in many countries, usually because of the risk of disease, but even our pack animals should be treated with distant respect. It's just not worth the risk.

Two hours later, after many breathless stops, we reach the top of the pass and are surrounded by a panorama of the entire mountain range. We're exhilarated at having made it although it's very cold and windy at the top and we're all having breathing difficulties. We stop for a group photograph and then start the long winding track downwards. This is the highest I've ever trekked and it instils in me a huge admiration for those who scale the world's major peaks. As we descend, I'm relieved at how much easier the walking gets with every step. The ever-decreasing altitude brings a sense of lightness as our lungs respond to the oxygen. We arrive at the banks of a fast-moving stream that flows down to the river and our guide tells me that we'll need to cross it two or three times because the path jumps the stream at various points.

There's a lot of talk among the crew about the appearance of the stream. Last night's rain has dramatically increased the flow and speed of the water, which normally is little more than a burbling brook. Over the next two and a half hours we find ourselves having to cross this fast-moving watercourse more than twenty times because the banks have washed away. At first all the men – both trekkers and crew – throw boulders into the water to form a makeshift 'bridge' for us to leap across but this is very time-consuming and physically exhausting. I'm still wearing the beautiful leather Italian hiking books that I bought two decades ago but luckily the rest of the group have more modern lightweight synthetic boots which cope with the water much better. The last ten crossings are done simply by walking through the knee-deep, fast-flowing stream. My boots become waterlogged and I can feel that my sodden socks are starting to rub the skin off my feet. This doesn't bode well for the long walk ahead.

Eventually we leave the stream behind and head for a small village where we're able to rest for a little while and have some lunch. Everyone's looking the worse for wear and I'm thankful that we had those three strong men in our group – I can't imagine how we would have coped with that last treacherous section without their help. It's taken the group several hours longer to reach our lunch spot than was planned.

At the village one of the women in the group alerts me to the fact that another group member is feeling extremely unwell. She's utterly exhausted and doesn't believe she can walk another step. We quickly organise a bed for her in a village house and our local guide manages to get enough coverage on his mobile phone to call for help. A vehicle will collect her and take her down to the river to wait for the group to catch up on foot. I hadn't realised that there was a road leading up to this village and am greatly relieved that we can get her out safely and comfortably. As we're already running well behind schedule, the lead guide heads off with the main group while I wait with our sick trekker and her friend for the transport to arrive. She sleeps soundly while we wait more than an hour for the small truck to arrive. It's a bumpy ride but from my perspective much better than allowing an exhausted trekker to walk. She feels hugely restored after her sleep.

We make it to the river ahead of the walkers, before I realise that we're not being collected by Jeeps on this side of the Indus. Instead, there's a large woven basket suspended above the river with thick cables. It's the only way the locals can get across and three people at a time are being scrunched up in the basket and hauled from one side of the raging river to the other. The Indus has also been affected by the rainfall and is very wild and muddy. It looks perilous but after what we have already been through today, I am sure everyone will take it in their stride.

Eventually I see the main group walking down the winding track towards us. They look extremely tired but relieved to be nearing the end of what's been a very long, tough day. Our local guide is talking on his mobile phone and looking very anxious.

He takes me aside to break the news that the vehicles that were booked to meet us and take us to our hotel can't get through because the road's been blocked by a massive land-slide. There's no alternative but to keep walking once when we get across the river. He tells me a team of workers are furiously trying to clear a section so that vehicles can get through, but it might take all night. We have to walk.

The human spirit is incredible when faced with adversity. The group accept with good grace that we have to continue on foot even though, by now, it's nearly 7pm and we have been walking for more than twelve hours. The light is fading and only a couple of us have torches in our daypacks. The road follows the river on one side with a steep embankment on the other. There are signs of several smaller landslides from this slope and the weather's turning bad again, with dark clouds threatening to bring more rain.

I sense danger but we have no choice but to keep going. I start singing as we trudge along, and the others join in. Even our trekker who was so unwell has rallied and is walking strongly. We've managed to draw on reserves of energy and courage we didn't know we had to keep pushing ourselves along this risky path. We had no idea when we set out in the early hours of this morning that we'd still be walking in complete darkness. Three hours later we reach a truck that's finally made it through the landslide. Wearily we clamber into the windowless container hold, sitting with our backs against the sides. Although I suspect that my feet are badly torn up because my socks and boots are still soaking wet from the river crossings, I'm just so relieved that everyone's safe and that soon we'll be able to eat and sleep. I'm dreaming of hot soup and a slug of brandy.

When we arrive at the hotel, well after 11pm, it's in darkness. They've given up on us and closed down for the night, in the belief we'd been entirely cut off by the landslide. We rouse some members of staff, who rush around heating up food for us. There's no brandy so we settle for a beer. I peel off my shoes and socks and am confronted by bloody shredded skin on the soles of my feet. I'll need to take care to avoid infection.

Our program for the following day is quite tight, but I insist there should be a late start to give people an extra couple of hours to recover.

At breakfast everyone's bright and bubbly, full of excited discussion about the previous day's big adventure. I never fail to be impressed at how well people cope in extreme situations. It's certainly one of the toughest circumstances I've faced with a group and yet everyone seems energised by it. I'm full of admiration for the way everyone's handled the long, hard day. It gives the term 'stepping outside your comfort zone' new meaning.

Several days later, back at our hotel in Leh, I read a news-paper account of the massive landslide back in 2010 that wiped out an entire village, killing more than 1000 people. It gives me pause for thought.

39

A house is found

Although we've agreed not to actively look for a house in the mountains until the farm and/or the cottage have been sold, Lynne's been keeping an eye on the market, checking every few days to see what sort of properties are coming up for sale and what the prices are like. They're keen to remain in Blackheath because that's where the children go to school, although she's also been looking at options on either side – Medlow Bath and Mount Victoria.

Late one afternoon she calls me: 'I know this isn't good timing, but I think I've found the right place for us.. Can you come and look at it at 9.30 tomorrow morning?'

The house has only just been listed that day and the agent had suggested we meet him at 11am because there was another couple viewing at 10am. Lynne insisted we could only come at 9.30am.

I drive over early with Eamonn and we wait outside the front gate for Ethan, Lynne and the agent to arrive.

It's a large brick house on the south side of the village, built in the 1920s and original apart from the addition of a timber veranda around two sides. Nestled in more than half an acre of land with old maple trees and a handmade drystone wall along the front, the house and its setting immediately capture my heart. We're all exchanging 'looks' as the agent shows us through. He tells us that the house has remained in the same family for nearly seventy years and has a heritage order on it which might limit any future external renovations. We love it, simple as that. On the spot we tell the agent we want it and go into a huddle to work out how we could slap a deposit down as quickly as possible.

Outside, the next couple are waiting for their turn to view the property. We have to lock it down, immediately.

We lock it down.

I go to the bank in Bathurst later that day and organise bridging finance for my half of the property. Ethan has a prospective buyer for their cottage and had planned on finishing the renovations first. Luckily they're able to do a deal to advance the sale of the house 'as is'. We can make it happen.

Everything happens very quickly. The loans are approved, the deposit's paid and the cottage is sold. Within three months the family have moved into the lovely old house and set up my room with a temporary futon bed so that I can stay overnight whenever I please. I still need to live at the farm with all my furniture in place until after it's been sold – houses lose a lot of their appeal when cold and empty. It makes me feel so secure knowing that we have a beautiful house that's exactly right for all our needs.

I can't wait to get stuck into the new garden.

40

Auction anxiety

Agreeing to put the farm up for auction adds to my anxiety levels. I'd much rather just put a price on it and wait for an offer but the agent is convinced I'll do better this way. I know that David would *never* have agreed to such an idea, because of the costs involved. I also believe he would have found an auction too stressful, but I allow myself to be persuaded.

Every Saturday the farm's open for inspection for several hours from midday. My grandson and I run around like mad things, making it look as fresh and pretty as we can. Flowers in every room, a slow-burning wood stove creating a cosy atmosphere. Smells of bread baking – this isn't a phony addition as I bake three times a week, regardless.

Five minutes before the agents are due to arrive we make ourselves scarce – usually treating ourselves to a hot lunch at the Tarana Pub, twenty minutes across country from the farm. I love this secluded village nestled in a lush valley, and its old pub that's become popular with weekend tourists. There's a wonderful covered deck with tables overlooking the rolling countryside and the historic, but seldom used, railway station. We sneak back home after 2pm and the agent always leaves a note on the kitchen table, saying how many prospective buyers have been through. Small numbers compared to city properties, but they keep reassuring me that there's genuine interest.

The auction isn't held on site but in swish rooms in Sydney. I find the prospect terrifying and Tony's wife Leslie comes into town to lend some moral support. I really have no idea how much the farm will fetch and that uncertainty makes it a gruelling process. I know the lowest limit I can accept but the agent has kept talking up the possibility of considerably more – and the price range varies by more than $250,000. How I wish David were here to deal with all this stuff.

The farm does sell at auction, but at the very lowest end of the price range. I'm a little disappointed but also hugely relieved it's all over. Now I can move forward to start my new and very different life. After all, it's only money.

I have three months to pack up and move. I haven't even looked into David's shed and I know this must be a priority, along with rehoming the livestock and working out what to do with all the 'stuff' we've accumulated over four decades.

There's an old car – a 1949 Mark V Jaguar David bought thirty-five years ago in a moment of madness. I drove it for five years until it failed rego and it's been sitting either in a garage or farm shed ever since. There are shelves of books to be culled – I only keep my favourites. Boxes of old sewing things are a great find: I keep my mother's old Singer and an unfinished patchwork quilt I started in the 1980s. Maybe I'll have time to finish it now. Old letters between David's parents will be returned to his sister – one day I even, bizarrely, find a Nazi officer's cap and cane from the Second World War. The cap has the brass eagle and swastika. I vaguely remember David telling me that his father, who was part of the New Zealand Expeditionary Forces mopping up in Italy after the war, was involved in a skirmish in which he shot and killed a Nazi official. He told me that his dad had souvenired the dead man's cap and cane – and here they are. David hadn't mentioned he'd brought these grisly relics to Australia, as he would have known how horrified I would be. I shudder. But what to do with them? Eventually I decide to offer them to the New Zealand National War Memorial.

Although it's nearly eighteen months since David died, I find getting rid of his clothing heart-wrenching. I keep his favourite things – a couple of hats, the jackets he took to the Cannes Film Festival; his treasured T-shirts. I've been sleeping with his three best-loved T shirts under my pillow.

Our three sons give up some weekends to help me tackle David's shed and I'm ruthless. I do give the boys the option of taking anything they fancy, but they have no need for 'stuff' either, although Aaron keeps a lot of his dad's film industry records, which otherwise are headed to the local tip. He carts off boxes and boxes of stuff. The ephemera of a life's work, all gone. It's cleansing.

One afternoon, sitting on the dusty floor of the shed, painstakingly going through an old cream filing cabinet and discarding most of the contents, I come across a file marked 'Private'. I start going through it and find several handwritten letters from me written at various times during our relationship. From time to time I was upset with David, usually because of his lengthy absences and his obsessive focus on his work at the expense of our family life. I have only hazy memories of writing to him out of frustration and anger. Obviously, we must have long ago resolved these issues, but why did he hang onto the letters all these years? It's quite painful to read them and I relegate them to the 'tip' pile. Nestled in the back of the same file is a cream envelope and I tip out the contents. There are numerous photographs of a very beautiful, naked woman. There are also letters from her. Love letters to David. I look at the dates and realise they span several years around the second decade of our marriage. I recognise her name: David mentioned her several times, describing her as 'an old girlfriend from New Zealand'. Again, I'm very hazy about all this but I think he mentioned that she was living in Darwin and that she'd been back in touch with him. It was a long time ago.

After my initial shock at this discovery, I start to laugh. I laugh and laugh until tears of laughter roll down my cheeks. I hold her letters and photographs to my chest, cherishing them. Finally, I understand. Finally, I get it. How David was able to so easily forgive me my wild few years; my love affair. He had obviously been in exactly the same position – in a relationship with someone else while married to me. Possibly in love with someone else while still in love with me. Wanting our marriage to survive but not wanting to let go of the other woman.

He must have known those letters were in the cabinet in the shed. Or had he forgotten about them? Maybe he wanted me to find them, knowing that I would not be hurt or angry. Knowing that I would understand.

Never have I loved David more than at this moment. I put her photographs and letters on the 'burn' pile.

Is an affair a reflection of an unhappy marriage or part- nership? It can be, but often it has nothing to do with it. In many instances an affair isn't premeditated. It's something that happens between people – a spark, eye contact, an acci- dental touch. Electricity, chemistry, call it what you will. I honestly had never contemplated an affair. Without being judgmental of others I was repelled by the idea because of the pain I knew my father's extramarital relationships had caused within my own family. When I discovered in my mid- teens that my father was having an affair with a woman we all knew I hated her and blamed her. I could never see myself being like that woman. It was unthinkable.

In my early fifties when I found myself attracted to another man and not resisting his advances, I was shocked at myself.

Surprised at my willingness to go along with what I sensed was a very bad idea. How did that work? The brain said one thing, the body responded differently. My inner dialogue during this period was chaotic because I was so confused and confronted by both my desires and my actions. I was not myself, or not the 'self' I imagined myself to be.

The reason our marriage survived was because we both really wanted to stay together and because we didn't stop loving each other in spite of everything that happened. Maybe it was helped by the fact that my affair happened on the other side of the world and not on our doorstep in Australia. I had attempted to neatly carve up my life into manageable portions. Here in Australia, home, husband and family could be loved and contained. In France, another world away, a lover. I would cry when I left France and yet be delighted to see David waiting for me at the airport in Australia. I still felt physically attracted to him, so there was never that issue of rejecting him or falling out of love. Just as I had juggled fulltime work and raising children for two decades, I thought I was juggling a marriage, my work and a lover with great aplomb. I was delusional, of course.

Things in our marriage never went back to the way they were before the affair. We had discovered a lot about each other, both good and bad, and this paved the way for a more open and honest relationship. It made us more thoughtful and considerate. We became better at listening to each other and we appreciated each other, and what we had, much more. Having so nearly been torn apart, we clung together ferociously.

Gradually the sheds begin to empty and animals are picked up and taken away by local farming friends. I give away so many things – bedding, furniture, paintings and posters of David's films. What's left, I store in a metal container that will be locked up and left on the bush block until I decide what to do with it. I have one more major obligation to perform – to plant out the 200 trees and shrubs along the banks of Frying Pan Creek. It's part of my contract with the water conservation group, and it makes me feel good knowing that I'm leaving this land in better shape than when we came here seventeen years ago.

I've always kept in contact with a small group of friends from my high school days. They offer to help with the planting and so, on one of my last weekends at the farm, they come up for a Sunday working bee. It really doesn't take as long as I feared to get all the tubestock native plants settled into the ground along the banks of the creek. I hope that there'll be some summer rains to keep them growing.

The rest of the move is done in just one day. We hire a small truck to take my pared-down possessions – a bed, a wardrobe, a chest of drawers, my clothes, my books and a small television and stereo system – from the old farm to the lovely brick house at Blackheath. Fundamentally I'm going from a sprawling five-bedroom house with two living and dining areas and a heritage community dance hall out the back, to one room. It's a big room – the original formal sitting room with a lovely bay window and an open fireplace. But it's just one room and I know it will be an adjustment. The ultimate in downsizing.

As I close the kitchen door at the back of the farmhouse for the last time, it's not with sadness but with a huge sense of relief. I have felt so personally responsible for the care and upkeep of this large place since the day David died. It's so costly keeping a property like this going, with its ageing infrastructure and ongoing problems with wild weather and water supply. It really has been weighing me down, so it's with a sense of lightness that I travel down the long drive and over the creek, heading for my new life.

41

A room of one's own

OCTOBER 2016

So now I have a room of my own. Every single thing in this room holds meaning for me. Nothing is purely decorative or functional, it's as though I have boiled my life down to a rich essence and here it is surrounding me. My love of textiles and colour is apparent. David once commented that I had created 'an Indian brothel' in our family room at the farm. Yes, I had collected some brilliant saris in New Delhi and sewn them into curtains. Embroidered cushions, rugs and a colourful floor pouffe added to the effect. Well, if that room was a brothel, this one is an entire red-light district! Chairs covered in fabric from Rajasthan, silk and tribal rugs, piles of books waiting for the bookshelves that Ethan will build for me. The massive portrait of a melancholy David that was entered in the Archibald takes up half a wall and I position it so that his downcast eyes gaze at the wardrobe and not me when I'm in bed.

As I place each conserved item in its new home – on the wall or over the fireplace – I'm cheered. This space is perfect for me and it really is all I need. I can work on my computer or listen to music or catch the evening news on my small television. I can read for hours – I have gradually regained the ability to enjoy novels after three years of lacking the focus or the inclination. Now I relish getting lost in a story again, especially one where the words nurture me.

The family have already been living in the house for six months and they've developed a strong feeling for how it will work to support three generations. The kitchen is a shared family space and Lynne proposes that rather than tripping over each other to prepare meals together we have specific nights when we each cook. Three nights for me; three nights for her and one night when Ethan and their oldest son, Caius, prepare 'Man Food'. Lynne will do the major shopping once a fortnight, keeping the pantry well-stocked with everything we need. On our designated cooking nights we choose whatever we fancy and buy what's necessary. This means I still have the pleasure of planning a meal and shopping for the hero ingredient, which I've always loved doing, something that everyone will enjoy, plus some of the children's absolute favourites. It's never a chore but a labour of love.

Originally there was only one bathroom, but one of the small bedrooms has been converted into a large family bathroom with specific features to make it easier to care for their oldest disabled child Isabella. This leaves the original bathroom for me to use. There's also an outside loo. I've always loved a house with an outside loo!

As my room was originally the main living room, we're making do with using the dining room next to the kitchen as our family room. However, Ethan and Lynne have been working on plans to submit to council that will extend the back of the house into a huge communal living and dining room. It will be furnished with my treasured furniture that's stored in the container.

The block of land is quite lovely, sloping with an open sunny area that will be ideal for our orchard and vegie garden; and a shady section of deciduous trees will form the basis of our ornamental garden. We're all keen gardeners – unlike me, they both have horticultural training – so I feel confident that we can achieve great things in this space. There's nothing better than youth and enthusiasm when creating a garden.

I start working on the new garden immediately. It's early in the season and I send off for nursery catalogues from my favourite perennial and rose growers – mostly in Victoria. We spend many hours together in the evenings, poring over these tempting glossy booklets then ordering the plants online. There's a large sunny section of lawn at the front of the house and I decide to create a perennial border there. I begin by watering it deeply, spreading cow manure then mulching to supress the grass. When the large boxes of tiny tubestock plants start being delivered, I draw a plan with taller growers at the back and low growers at the front. I've never been rigid in my gardening practices – I'm a bit chaotic and quite prepared to move things around if they don't look quite right. For me, gardening has to be fun or it's simply not rewarding. I don't ever see the garden as a 'chore'. It's my happy place and I know it will play such an important part in my healing process.

In my new life, the perfect day is a cup of tea before starting very early in the garden, gradually getting more and more filthy and dishevelled as I work my way through the various newly planted beds. I have a small transistor radio in a basket with my hand tools, tuned to the classic music channel. I like to cook myself a little hot lunch – an omelette or pasta – and eat outside with a glass of wine. Then another hour in the garden, mostly tidying and putting things away, followed by a bath and an hour on my bed, reading. Invariably I have a short snooze. In the evening if there's a chill in the air I light my little wood fire, pour more wine and watch the early news. Cook dinner if it's my turn, in which case someone else cleans up. Indeed, the cooperative teenage boy in the house rinses the plates and pots and stacks the dishwasher every single night.

I don't watch television drama very much; mostly current affairs and maybe comedy if it's on. Usually I read again for a few hours then turn out the lights.

My first undertaking, apart from the garden, is to wean myself off the antidepressant drugs and I do so under the eye of my new GP, a woman I've known for more than thirty years during my previous time in the Mountains. I do it gradually and suffer no backlash. Immediately I start to feel more clear-headed and in control. The medication helped me tremendously during a time when I was overwhelmed but I no longer need it.

When I turn out the light at night, snug in our old bed with David's T-shirts still under the pillow, I feel safe. Not safe from any imagined threat or danger; just safe in my surroundings. I haven't felt like this, in truth, since David died. It's such a good feeling. I am safe.

42

Loving reunions

One unexpected bonus of moving back to the mountains has been reconnecting with many old friends with whom I'd lost touch. I spent so much of the last two decades travelling and writing, I'd gradually drifted away from those connections made while our children were growing up. I have friends here that date back to the mid-1970s when we first moved up from Sydney; our children went to preschool together, then infants, primary and all through high school. Most of our children moved away for their tertiary education, but some, like Ethan and Lynne, have started returning to this area to raise and educate their own children.

My first connection is an invitation to join a book group. Amazingly, it's the same book group that my mother Muriel belonged to more than thirty-five years ago and I'm delighted to find it still going strong. I didn't join when I was younger because I was working under pressure and never seemed to have the time to read the book, let alone attend the meeting. In any event I thought it was good for Mum to have some outside activities of her own as a respite from our noisy family life. I'm thrilled to see everyone again – there are several new faces but the core of the group has remained the same. Here we all are, many of us now grandmothers, looking at the world from the other end of the tunnel. There's no doubt age has brought us wisdom and we have lively and often outrageous conversations, not just about literature but about life. It's a morning meeting and we all bring food to share. Often the gathering spills over past lunchtime as we thrash out our ideas and opinions. I always leave elated and thankful for the gift of friendship.

The half-finished patchwork quilt that I found at the back of the linen cupboard when I was clearing out the farm has travelled with me to Blackheath, along with my mother's heavy black 1952 Singer sewing machine. It's been so long since I tackled the making of an elaborate quilt that I've completely forgotten the tricks and techniques. One of the book club friends also belongs to a patchwork group so I join up and take my forgotten project along to finish. Several of the women are also friends from the good old days and we sit around a huge table drinking tea, eating cake, sewing and talking. It's so soothing, so calming to sew and talk. It's creative too, and I rediscover forgotten artistic skills. I've collected so many fabrics on my travels, and after I finish the traditional quilt I search for unusual patterns and fabric combinations. My quilts are bright coloured in geometric designs. It's good for me to slow down and piece these collected fabrics together. It's very precise with no room for mistakes, and I find this discipline positive as I am by nature a full-speed-ahead person, somewhat impatient and wanting to get things done quickly. With quilting you need to develop a methodical approach and there's also a lot of mathematical skill involved, which is good for the old brain. I smile to myself, remembering sitting in the bar in my French village at lunchtime, drinking numerous pitchers of chilled rosé in the summer sun; here, I'm sipping tea and sewing. *C'est la vie!*

I've also become a community volunteer, spending several hours a week with a delightful woman in her late nineties who still lives at home and cooks for herself. Betty has a supportive family living nearby and my contribution is to spend some quality time with her, just having fun. We often go to a film, sometimes we go shopping and sometimes we just hang out in the local café with a milkshake. She has become a dear friend, I love our conversations tremendously and having an extra person in my life to care for is very satisfying indeed. It's a two-way street: we both benefit from our get-togethers and the laughter we inevitably share.

Blackheath is a village rather than a suburb and has a cohesive and lively community feel about it. There's always something happening – tango lessons in the pub and Saturday afternoon jazz (in the other pub). There's a history forum in the summer; an excellent independent bookshop that hosts many book launches and literary events and every spring a rhododendron festival with a street parade. There's a community farm garden where volunteers work on a Sunday and enjoy the produce they've grown. I was worried at first that going back to the mountains might be like stepping backwards in time, trying to recapture something long lost – I feel a need to keep moving forwards as my life has changed so much. But being here absolutely feels like moving forwards. I can be as quiet as I like, working in the garden all day or bushwalking around the escarpment, or I can kick my heels up in one of the village pubs. It's a balance.

Now that I've settled in my new home and my finances have been sorted I can also start to plan for future mountain treks and visits to France. While I want to spend most of my time here with the family, cooking and working in the garden, I'm undoubtedly drawn to new adventures. I've kept all my old laptop computers holding the photographs from various expeditions over a twenty-year period and I have enough time now to look back over these images and relive some of the experiences from the past. I've already made plans to revisit Morocco with a group in the spring and to walk Ladakh again – probably with another yoga crowd.

The photographs that really stand out for me are of Mongolia, a place I visited in 2010 with a large group of trekkers keen to know more about the botany of this extraordinary country. Thinking about that journey takes me back to a time long before David was diagnosed, when my life and our future together seemed so certain.

Looking through the images from that incredible journey inspires me to get a group together for a repeat visit, especially as it seems likely that the nomadic way of life there is about to change dramatically. More than thirty per cent of the population are nomadic and their lifestyle is now under threat as a result of climate change. Drought, overgrazing (fuelled by wealthy countries' passion for cashmere), and uncontrolled mining have all affected the groundwater and the alpine ecosystems.

Unless work can be done to conserve water in the alpine grazing regions, and the size and spread of herds kept to a strict limit, this way of life may well disappear – perhaps even in my lifetime. So I work with World Expeditions to put together an itinerary to see how it's changed in the last nine years.

43

A fascinating destination

My decision to explore Morocco and take groups back with me each year has been a good one. Each time I return I view this fascinating country with new eyes and I have been collecting and reading books on its people, history and culture. This year I have two small groups; one doing the original itinerary that includes all the major cities – Casablanca, Rabat, Meknes, Fes and Marrakech and a second group going to the Sahara and the coastal city of Essaouira.

Smaller groups work well for my philosophy of travel. Not only does it encourage a bonding as there is an opportunity for everyone to really get to know each other; it simply makes the logistics of getting around so much faster and easier.

I have a disdain for large-scale mass tourism, not just because of the impact to the environment and on the people who are unfortunate enough to live in popular international destinations, such as Venice or Rome. It's also the quality of the experience for the tourists themselves when being herded around in their hundreds. It's impossible to really get a strong feeling for a place you are visiting when you are seeing it from the comfort of a seat in a bus with sixty other people. Imagine the time spent just waiting for a lunch or toilet stop, especially if there is a convoy of two or three buses doing the same tour. It feels like a nightmare to me.

I always include walking as an integral part of every tour. On the ground, on foot, we gain a stronger insight into where we are and how it all works. Interactions with people and animals and the way a place feels and smells, all our senses need to be involved to try and understand and appreciate. Instead of looking down and out from behind a pane of glass we are in the midst of it. Part of it but not in an overwhelming or invasive sense. Given the size of the tourist industry world-wide it's becoming increasingly difficult to 'tread lightly' but I am determined to continue venturing out with an attitude of keeping it small and low-key.

Perhaps the most profound revolution I have observed over the decades is the intrusion of the internet and social media in travel. During my early years we were often completely out of range of all communication in regions where villagers lived without electricity and relied on news and messages being conveyed by word of mouth. Gradually satellite dishes started popping up and this of course brought tremendous improvements in the life and safety of those living in remote regions.

However for tourists surely the opportunity of leaving behind some of our sophisticated modern habits should be relished. A time to button off Facebook and Twitter and switch over to observation and learning.

Day one of a trip when we all meet our local guide and driver for the first time, I feel a need to remind people to maximise their enjoyment and memories of the places we will see by not viewing the entire trip through the lens of a camera or a phone. We will recall what we have seen with our eyes and heard with our ears much more vividly than anything we might capture on a smart phone. In Morocco there is so much to soak up and absorb. In each Imperial city we have a specialised local guide willing to share a wealth of knowledge and insight. This year, for the first time, two of these guides are local women and this adds an entirely new perspective. In a group such as ours we have the privilege of being able to hear every word that is spoken and to ask questions. It's a rich and enduring exchange.

The icing on the cake is spending some time in the High Atlas Mountains, staying for three nights or more in a Berber village house and doing day walks through the fields and over the high peaks from where the views are sublime. Following the locals on donkeys to a Sunday market and buying fresh fruit for our picnic lunch by the river. I treasure these moments for their gentle pace and calming mood. Surely travel doesn't need to be all rush and bustle? Slow food, slow gardening, slow travel. Bliss. Very few tourists up here; no buses, no traffic, no worries.

The trip down to the Sahara is my first and quite an eye opener. It takes two days by small bus and then four-wheel drive to reach the dunes, but it's worth the time spent for the views. At the suggestion of our local guide we only carry in sufficient gear for overnight and although we are given comfortable tents with proper beds I view the episode as camping. Late afternoon we arrive in time for mint tea before heading up to the highest dune to gaze at the setting of the sun. The stillness and the fading light captivate us. It's another moment that will stay with me.

Sahara sand is powder fine and invasive. Our drivers wrap our heads in traditional scarves and we quickly appreciate the practical benefit of this, shielding our ears, noses and mouths from the insidious fine golden sand. It seems to be everywhere – in my pockets, my socks, eyebrows, and down my knickers.

We sleep deeply in our warm tents and leave for the Atlantic coast the following morning, on the way staying overnight at an astonishing old 'resort' and having a hammam (a traditional steam bath) where we strip naked and are scrubbed from head to toe by gorgeous women who delight in throwing buckets of steaming hot water over our heads. I absolutely love it and feel cleaner that I have ever felt in my life. It gives soaking up the experience a new dimension.

Travel in this sense opens our minds and hearts to other worlds. It's such a beautiful feeling, not standing on the outside looking in but jumping in, boots and all.

44

Ageing outrageously

I have mixed feelings about growing older. The 'good' me understands and accepts the inevitability of the process and embraces each year that arrives as if my entire life has been leading up to this moment. Instead of lamenting the loss of beauty and strength, the positive me enjoys not having the same work pressures and expectations and revels in accumulated wisdom. Cares less about being judged or criticised.

The 'bad' me looks in the mirror and curses. She looks at the back of her once-pretty hands and sees brown spots and purple veins, then gets cranky when she can't remember the name of a close friend.

Although very male-centric, I loved Daniel Klein's book *Travels with Epicurus* in which he examines ageing in the context of old people enjoying their lives on a Greek island.

Here, friendships and companionship make ageing a joy. Eating and drinking together, talking, laughing, reminiscing. Reading the book, I did sometimes wonder what the old women were doing while the old men were enjoying themselves so much (probably slaving away in the kitchen), however the conclusion he reaches is hard for me to disagree with: 'Old age is a privilege to be savoured, rather than a disease to be cured or a condition to be denied'.

A lot depends, of course, on your situation. Poverty and/or lack of family support can make growing older a nightmare. To finish a life waiting to die in a poor-quality nursing home is everyone's worst fear. Sickness is also a huge negative, as our bodies age and wear down we often need medication just to maintain a basic quality of life. I'm frightened of reaching that stage when I can no longer drive my car and lose my independence and mobility. I worry about friends who live alone becoming socially isolated and frail.

For me, the trick is to stay active and curious and to keep going forward. Having something to look forward to helps – a trip, a holiday or a gathering of old friends. It's fun to reminisce, especially with younger family members around. I love showing my grandchildren old photographs and telling them about this or that relative or what it felt like living in a particular era. They still don't really believe we were nearly teenagers by the time we had television and that life before mobile phones was perfectly okay.

I garden most days and insist on doing the mowing of our large garden and the wide street verges because it's a better way of keeping fit than going to a gym. I try to keep my brain buzzing with lots of reading and following the news. I stay passionate about causes and continue to shout at politicians on the television when they say something stupid. This happens a lot.

I love my 'quiet thinking times' – unless it's at three in the morning, when I'd rather be fast asleep. It's delicious to stay in bed for a few minutes before getting up, just lying there and remembering different times that stand out in my life – when I was a single girl, starting my first job. What it felt like to fall in love, to be pregnant and to breastfeed. Different sexual moments. When I was in the midst of my love affair and constantly doing naughty things. At the time when I was taking those risks I remember thinking to myself 'at least you'll have something to look back on with a smile'. That's exactly what has happened. The time I sneaked a man into my room at a posh London club – not once, but two nights in a row. Shopping online for saucy underwear: a suspender belt and stockings which I wore on a crowded suburban train to meet my lover. Having sex on a car bonnet and losing my knickers in the woods. These were things I should have been doing in my teenage years; not my fifties!

In her mid-seventies my mother used to say she still felt exactly the same on the inside and always got a fright when she saw herself in the mirror. I don't feel like that at all. Since David died I feel like a much more mature woman. That experience alone has shaped how I see myself and my place in the world. I can still have fun and be outrageous; I can dance at a party with the best of them. I simply no longer feel completely carefree.

When I first told my friends and other family members that I was planning to live in a sharehouse with my youngest son and his family, there was a mixed reaction. Most were hugely enthusiastic, especially those who had known me for a long time and also knew our family structure back in Leura when my mother was living with us. They understood how we could make an extended family work; not a granny flat out the back but a properly integrated three-generational home.

One friend, however, was concerned and asked:

'But what if you meet someone; what if you want to start a new relationship? Won't living in this share house make it very difficult?'

The idea hadn't entered my mind, even for a moment. I suppose my friend was trying to consider every angle from my perspective. Buying a house with other family members means that effectively my assets are completely tied up and it would be difficult and messy to leave this situation and set up another home independently. Also, there's the logistics of entering into another relationship while living in a family home where there are young children. Granny lurching back from the local pub with a bloke on her arm may not be very seemly.

In fact on the day that I moved in to my room here at Black-heath, and my wide wooden sleigh bed was assembled and made up with fresh sheets, my then five-year-old grandson Owynn bounced into the middle of the big European pillows and commented: 'This is a very big bed, Mutie.'

(Mutie is the grandmother name given to me when the first grandchild was born twenty-five years ago.)

'You know this bed,' I reminded him. 'It's Granddad's and my bed from the farm. You often used to climb into this bed so I could read you a story.'

He pondered for a moment, then patted one side of the bed – David's side of the bed. 'You could have mens in here,' he suggested.

Not a man but *mens*, plural! The mental image of me staggering back from the pub with a man on each arm doesn't even bear thinking about.

I haven't really contemplated a new relationship for several reasons. First and foremost, I feel quite satisfied with what I had over those forty-three years. Maybe it's rare, but I feel as though I've been so thoroughly and unwaveringly loved that I simply don't need to go looking for that again. I greatly doubt I could ever find anyone who would love me and tolerate me the way that David did, decade after decade. I shudder at the thought of being in a partnership with someone who only half-loved me; who criticised me or got angry with me. Who shouted at me. Falling in love is very exciting and I am sad to think that I may never have that feeling again. I have fallen in love three times in my life and it was thrilling in every way. Yet there's a lot more to a partnership than that initial electrifying buzz of new love: it has to sustain and support and nurture. It's just too much to expect from anyone.

There's also the practical reality of ageing and health. I'm now in my late sixties and any prospective partner would most probably be in the same age group or maybe even older. It's a dangerous age, especially for men, it seems. I can't imagine watching another man I care for dying before my eyes. That feeling of helplessness in the face of decline. I loved David so much and caring for him during those two years was a great privilege but at times so very difficult, so heartbreaking and emotionally exhausting. The same would apply if I were to become sick, and needed that care from somebody new in my life. Imagine having to physically and emotionally support a dying person that you didn't have a really powerful connection with. It would be gruelling for you both.

I look back with satisfaction on the relationships I've had, knowing they can never be replicated.

'Never say never,' my friend added after I tried explaining my attitudes to her. I laughed.

Of course, there's also companionship and sex. I haven't abandoned my desire for intimacy and there's a man I have a delightfully uncomplicated relationship with that includes lots of dinners and sleepovers. He doesn't yearn for a permanent partner; neither do I. We are not possessive and we don't really discuss our relationship at all. It just exists and that's enough. Conversation, food, wine and sex. The icing on the cake.

I'll keep meeting new people and leading walking tours as long as my legs will carry me. I'll keep cooking and gardening and hanging out with my family and friends and behaving badly whenever the opportunity arises.

Like David, I will not go gentle into that good night.

Epilogue

During the writing of this book many things happened that didn't make it into print. Darling people died who will be always missed, including Michael Laurence the actor and scriptwriter who was one of our oldest friends. My French neighbour and confidant Lucienne Hayter died in her nineties with the grace that epitomised her entire life. Robert Jones, the treasured husband of my friend Marilla North, left well before his time, creating a hole in our arts community. My long-time friend and book club member Di England died – her contribution to our lively discussions will be genuinely missed. Most significantly for our family, Ethan and Lynne's beautiful daughter Isabella Rosa, who would have been seventeen in January 2019, died in the October before her birthday. There are no words to describe how profoundly we all feel her loss.

Acknowledgements

I am fortunate indeed to be part of a very warm and funny family. Their love and support through good and bad times has been fantastic. My grandchildren make me smile and give me hope for the future. Sue Badyari, Kate Harper and Kate Baker of World Expeditions/UTracks have supported my passion for adventure all the way. The ABC production team for *Gardening Australia* – the crews, the researchers and my fellow presenters – made that decade of my life exciting and fulfilling. My dear friend and colleague Christine Whiston; the outrageous Rose Lambeth and Helen Tharme, plus my many trekking friends and guides. Thanks to my long-time agent Lyn Tranter who first set me on the path of memoir-writing and also Fiona Henderson and all at Simon & Schuster who collaborated to make sure it all happened. Nick A'Hern for his enthusiastic creative input into our lives. My old and new friends here in the Blue Mountains who have welcomed me back into the community and my eternal school friends who kept an eye on me when times were tough. I take nothing for granted.

About the author

Mary Moody trained as a journalist at the *Australian Women's Weekly* in the 1960s. In the 1970s she moved to the Blue Mountains with her young family and became a passionate organic gardener. She wrote and edited countless gardening books and magazines, and was a presenter on the ABC's top rating *Gardening Australia* for ten years.

In 2000 Mary spent six months living alone in a medieval village in southwest France. At the end of her sabbatical she bought a house nearby that she still visits every year. She wrote four memoirs about her experiences, including the bestselling *Au Revoir* and *Last Tango in Toulouse*.

Today she leads horticultural tours in France, Morocco and the Himalayas. After the death of her husband David Hannay in 2014, Mary moved back to the Blue Mountains where she is developing a large garden in an extended family home with her son and his family. She has eleven grandchildren.